Rum & Reggae

Hans Offringa

Rum & Reggae

Conceptual Continuity

© 2013
Hans Offringa
Conceptual Continuity

Photography: Hans Offringa, Becky Lovett Offringa
Design & Layout: Becky Lovett Offringa
Cover Design: Studio Baat
Contributing Editors: Carsten Vlierboom, Erik Voskamp,
and Gert Jan van der Weerd
Consultants: Jan Beek, Dave Broom

ISBN 978-90-78668-26-8

www.hansoffringa.com
www.thewhiskycouple.com

To Ed and David

– the brothers –

Table of Contents

FOREWORD

Foreword

Some time ago I received a message from Dave Broom, my "distilled" friend. I deliberately use the word "distilled" since he is not only an excellent whisky writer but because his work on rum shows he is as passionate on that subject as on whisky. Dave asked if I wanted to spend some time with a man called Hans Offringa and philosophise with him about rum. "Of course" I replied, "it is my job after all, talking about rum and converting rum ideas into a liquid substance. It will be a pleasure to make time for Hans."

Not long thereafter a mildly wild and very passionate writer enters our rum paradise with a plan about a book that combines rum and reggae...

Until that very moment the thought had never crossed my mind, although it obviously could have, since I am not only a rum blender but also Honorary Consul of Jamaica for the Netherlands.

Step by step we dissolve ourselves into rum, the production, where it is made, how to produce that one version liked so much by the consumer, by blending various expressions of the drink. And yes, that is precisely what we've been doing for a long time.

Rum has been a major and important distillate for centuries. Its history is fascinating, marinated in romance, war and pirate stories. Rum played and still does play a foremost role in the history of the producing islands and in the many battles fought over territories. History shows the beauty of rum in traditions, storytelling and the many places on earth where it is currently produced.

Our company E&A Scheer has been part of that history for more than three centuries. Over time we developed ourselves from a trading company in products from remote places into a top player in the world of bulk rum. This by-product of cane sugar, still imported from far away countries, remains our main activity.

The volumes are large and the variation enormous. Whether it is rum we blend for use as a mixer, a cocktail ingredient, an after dinner drink or an essence for rum raisins, ice cream, chocolate or tobacco, E&A Scheer makes an appropriate blend for all these types of products.

Hans and I philosophise about a Jamaican rum blend, one that should fit a book called *Rum & Reggae*. We will succeed; there are so many interfaces. Then, suddenly, we talk in-depth about Jamaica, the land of rum but also very much the land of reggae. I've been travelling to that beautiful island for years and fell in love with this remarkable country and its people.

The motto on the crest of Jamaica is "out of many one people", referring to a blend of people from very different nations and continents who, in the course of history, were brought to Jamaica and formed into the people they now are. In my capacity as Honorary Consul I confer with many among them. They are a distinctive group, with a distinctive rhythm and cannot be compared to anyone else.

Is it there that they connect with reggae? That distinctive after beat, that unique rhythmic style? Inimitable, a blend of various rhythms, originated in Jamaica and then conquering the world!

Is that why Jamaican rum has such a distinctive taste? Very typical, usually a blend of various expressions of light and heavy rums, sometimes aged, loved by Jamaicans, but loved by many other people, too!

It is obvious to me. I love blending and I love a fine blend of products, whether it is a rum blend that fits from each dimension or a musical mix, say melody, which just sounds good. The combination of Rum & Reggae as described by Hans Offringa in this book is top notch.

Reading this book I not only encounter nice to know and need to know facts but also many acquaintances in Jamaica. A description of Good Hope Plantation, the place I stayed with my wife for a week, just after we had been married on the island. The story of Worthy Park and the people I met during the years I assisted them with building a new distillery on that beautiful estate of the Clarke family.

And, no doubt, Bob Marley, a legend for almost every Jamaican. His role in the development and the growth of reggae worldwide is undisputed.

Rum & Reggae, Rum & Jamaica, Drinks & Music. How wonderful and harmonious these combinations sound. And frankly, that is only very logical.

Carsten Vlierboom
Master Blender E&A Scheer and Honorary Consul
of Jamaica in the Kingdom of the Netherlands

INTRODUCTION

Introduction

Early in 2007 I developed a plan with my dear mentor and friend Michael Jackson, the beer and whisky writer: a plan to write about whisky and music. It didn't take long before we agreed on the topic – single malts and jazz. Not surprisingly so, since we shared a passion for both. It also suited my planned series of books about whisky and the senses. After having published *A Taste of Whisky*, dealing with Nosing and Tasting, I know could bend my ear to Listening.

Sadly Michael unexpectedly died that same year in August, just after he had witnessed the birth of *A Taste*, for which he had written a beautiful foreword. His reflections on and suggestions for my jazzy plan were luckily still there. To have his echo resound in my next book I dedicated *Whisky & Jazz* to him and published the English edition in 2009. Our mutual friend Dave Broom kindly wrote the foreword this time.

Book signing gigs followed in Charleston, Chicago and New York, accompanied by live jazz. Later that year, back in Europe, I also presented a Dutch edition. Upon my return in the USA I started to do additional research into the world of bourbon. First Becky and I went to Charleston to participate in the annual blues festival and the thought instantly occurred to me to work on something combining those two American icons. Before I realised, I was side-tracked from the whisky-and-senses road, instead on the road to a new series about drinks and music. This time Jim Rutledge, longstanding master distiller of Four Roses bourbon, offered to write the foreword and be my contributing editor as well. The Kentucky Bourbon Festival 2011 witnessed the launch of *Bourbon & Blues*, amidst a crowd of enthusiasts at Four Roses Distillery.

And, as is my modus operandi, shortly thereafter I presented a Dutch edition, this time travelling through my native country with two blues musicians on the Four Roses Bourbon & Blues Tour.

Now that I had succeeded in combining two favourite domains for a second time, I could not have been happier. However, my readers supplied me with some constructive criticism. Where they thought the paperback *Bourbon & Blues* very digestible, a large group among them considered the coffee table style book *Whisky & Jazz* beautiful, but too abstract in content and design. They also thought the whisky part was a bit shallow. I listened to my readers and decided to rewrite the book and turn it into story telling, instead of a showcase. I also considerably expanded the section about distilling.

Since 2012 it has been available in print as a paperback and in a Kindle version, albeit under a slightly different title, *Malts & Jazz*, to prevent confusion with the coffee table book. I thank my readers for their remarks because they challenged me to improve my writing. As an extra the Kindle edition has hyperlinks to the actual music on YouTube. When reading you can jump out of the story, listen and look at the musician and song described, then return.

In the mean time, thanks to Dave, I became more and more interested in rum and the alliteration with reggae was simply too good to ignore. In the back of my mind I had been playing with the idea of writing a trilogy, like *Lord of the Rings*, but without the Ring. I parked my idea about completing the series about whisky and the senses, following my ears and nose. Soon I discovered that the world of rum and reggae was not confined to Jamaica, where both domains met and joined, but spread out over a vast area.

Everywhere in the world rum has been made, for hundreds of years. Reggae in its current form has only existed for slightly more than half a century. Yet this musical style can be heard on all continents and is as widespread as rum, with a similarly dedicated group of followers. However, during our research I came upon another aspect that clearly illustrates, at least to me, that again I had combined two domains in a way that seems so logical in hindsight.

Reggae icon Bob Marley was made famous by the white Jamaican/Englishman Chris Blackwell, founder and one time owner of the Island record label that once contracted so many other well known musicians, among whom, Emerson, Lake & Palmer, Fairport Convention, Roxy Music, Traffic and U2.

Bob Marley was born out of a union between an Englishman and a Jamaican woman, whose ancestors came from Africa. They were taken to work the sugar plantations of Jamaica and other West-Indian islands. Sugar cane for rum, because that's what started it all.

Chris Blackwell's mother descended from Sephardic Jews who fled from Portugal in the 17th century and established themselves in the Caribbean, eventually making their fortune in rum. See? That is no coincidence when you research a book on rum & reggae. No, that is conceptual continuity!

And now, my trilogy on Drinks & Music is finished. *Rum & Reggae* is no ordinary tasting and listening guide. Again it is story telling, based on historical facts, interviews and personal observations. The main characters are Jamaica, Sugar and Riddim. Very digestible ones, I hope!

Hans Offringa
Charleston/Zwolle, Spring 2013

JAMAICA

Jamaica

Parliamentary monarchy:
Independent from Great Britain since 1962
Head of State: Queen Elizabeth II
Capital: Kingston
Size: almost 11,000 square kilometres
Inhabitants: approximately 3 million
Official language: English
Religion: mainly Protestant

Jamaica is the third largest and well known of the archipelago called Caribbean, consisting of nearly 7,000 islands and islets. Only Cuba and Hispaniola, the latter divided into the Dominican Republic and Haiti, are larger.

This group of islands came into existence due to a series of underwater volcanic eruptions, about 60 million years ago. During the millennia Jamaica developed into a green, mountainous island, cross-sectioned by over 120 rivers, partly above and partly underground. Only one of them, the Black River, can be navigated to a certain extent. A ring consisting of coral limestone surrounds the shore.

The island itself has large tracts of limestone, mainly in the so-called Cockpit Country. This part of Jamaica stretches from the northwest under Montego Bay to the southeast near Kingston, where one can find the highest peak of the area. When flying across, one can seen many green "holes", created by erosion and then largely covered by green vegetation. The highest point on the island is Blue Mountain Peak, searing almost 7,500 foot above sea level.

Around the year 650 the first people settled on the island, probably since it is pretty far away from the mainland. They might have come from Guyana and Venezuela and were Indians belonging to the Arawak tribes.

These early inhabitants called their new habitat Xaimayca, meaning "land of many water falls". It was a rowdy neighbourhood at the time, since they had to defend themselves regularly against attacks of another tribe: the Caribs, who, according to legend, saw no harm in eating their defeated opponents.

No wonder Columbus, who discovered the island in 1494 during his second trip to the Caribbean, did not receive a warm welcome by the remaining Arawaks when he tried to land on the northeast coast of Jamaica. He sailed westward where his second attempt to disembark appeared more successful. He conquered the island in the name of the Spanish king. Discovery Bay reminds us of those days.

The Spanish expected to find gold but this turned out to be a disappointment. As a colony, Jamaica didn't play a major role at the time, although the island was used extensively to stock weapons and food for the Spanish galleons. The foreign occupants cultivated part of the shore by introducing bananas and citrus fruits. They also imported horses, pigs and cows.

The indigenous Arawaks were skilfully and systematically exterminated, as was the habit of the Spanish oppressors in those days. Since they needed manual labour, they started to import slaves from West Africa as early as 1517.

Slowly the Spaniards lost their interest in the island, resulting in Jamaica becoming a plaything for other colonial oppressors, among whom the Portuguese, English, Dutch and French. Sudden attacks came as no surprise since in Europe the same countries were involved in constant battle. The Spaniards lacked enforcements from the homeland and eventually the English took Jamaica, in 1655.

That had not been an easy undertaking. Nearly three years after the last Spanish soldiers and citizens had fled to Cuba, there would be fights with the abandoned slaves, who had found shelter deep inland. Their descendants were called Maroons and are still considered a separate ethnic entity in Jamaica (in 1793 the English granted them limited independence, but that was taken from them after a huge slave revolt, in which conflict they sided with the "rebels").

Port Royal became the home port of many English, French and Dutch privateers. These "gentlemen" were captains of ships owning a decree from their homeland government to make life hell for the Spaniards. In fact piracy was made legal.

The crew were often called buccaneers, referring to poachers who stole stray pigs and cows from the uninhabited inner parts of the islands. The word stems from the French "boucan", loosely translated as "barbecue", since they had the habit of grilling the stolen animals over a metal grill. Plainly these buccaneers were straight pirates.

One of their most famous, or infamous if you prefer, specimens was Henry Morgan, after whom Captain Morgan rum is named.

How thin the dividing line between straightforward piracy and stealing-with-a-grant-from-your-governor is, can be illustrated by the following story. Morgan returned to Port Royal in 1671 with a huge loot and hundreds of Spanish prisoners of war. That was a bit too aggressive, since England and Spain had signed the Treaty of Madrid the year before, agreeing to end the hostilities between both countries. Now the Jamaican governor was rather embarrassed by Morgan's "good deed" and decided to send him to London in captivity, as a token of good will to Spain. As soon as Morgan was back in England he was knighted for his heroic behaviour and asked to return to Jamaica as lieutenant governor. Apparently the English government preferred to keep the cunning pirate at bay.

Just like the Spaniards, the English did not find gold on Jamaica, but instead they discovered fertile soil, suited to grow sugar cane, a crop that had been introduced to the Caribbean by Columbus about a century and a half earlier. The climatological conditions in the area appeared to be ideal for growing. The English, already owning more islands in the wider region, didn't hesitate. Experienced in growing sugar cane since 1640, on the more easterly located island of Barbados, they now had 30 times more surface to put to work.

In 1661 the first governor had been installed on the island and enterprising English were encouraged to leave the mother country to settle in Jamaica. From that time the first written evidence shows up that rum was made out of molasses, a by-product that is created during the refining of sugar from the cane juice.

It does not mean that Jamaica was the first island to produce rum or a liquid resembling it, but by its relative size it became the designated place for the English to grow sugar cane, with all the consequences for the world of distilled spirits in general.

By dedicated cultivation and growth of plantations, Jamaica would develop into the largest sugar-producing nation in the world during the 18th century. At the time hundreds of sugar factories, often combined with rum distilleries, dotted the surface of the island. Many remains can be found today, such as ruins of chimneys and windmills. Before the 18th century, sugar still was a luxury good, but it changed into a mass production and consumption article in the 19th century. The foundation for many an English sugar fortune however, was laid in the 17th century.

The occupier also introduced the English government and judicial system. The island became very important for the British economy. In order to grow and harvest sugar cane, huge numbers of manual labourers were necessary and they were "found" in West Africa. Slave traders made a web of journies, more commonly known as the triangle trade. The first leg went from Europe to Africa for acquiring slaves. The second one - or Middle Passage - from the West African coast to the Caribbean, where slaves were sold to plantation owners. Then the ship would return to

England, holding sugar and rum and other exports from the colonies in its hull. At the same time a lively trade was maintained between the Carribean and New England, from where corn and dried, salted fish were imported to feed the slaves. The salted fish by the way remains a well-loved dish in the Jamaican kitchen. The return cargo contained molasses for Boston, New York and New Jersey, creating an important rum industry in situ. The rum produced there was in its turn taken to West Africa and used for buying new slaves, after which a new trip over the Atlantic to the Caribbean was made.

As a side effect of the War of Independence (1775-1783) imports to North America became virtually impossible and the British put a great deal of force into guarding their belongings in the Caribbean.

On the other islands many slaves were put to labour as well. Their working conditions were so poor that problems were inevitable. In 1795 the first huge slave revolt in Jamaica took place, in Trelawney Town, lead by the Maroons. At first they booked considerable successes but a year later the rebels were slain. They were punished by means of exile to Nova Scotia. Used to the subtropical heat of Jamaica, they acclimated poorly to the bitter cold of their new habitat and were subsequently relocated to Sierra Leone. Today the latter country still harbours descendants of the Maroons.

More revolts would follow, time and again suppressed by the hard and cruel hand of the usurpers. In Europe however, ideas were changing, influenced by the French Revolution and the Enlightenment. In 1808 England officially abandoned the slave trade and made it unlawful. This dripped through to Jamaica, causing even more revolts, since slavery in itself was still allowed.

The St James Revolt around Christmas 1831 is recorded as the most important and largest one. It was lead by a former slave and reverend, Sam Sharpe. Again the rebels were bloodily slain and as a fearful example Sharpe was hanged by the neck on the central square at Montego Bay.

Fortunately the cries for abandoning slavery grew louder and louder, even among the planters themselves. In 1838 England passed the Emancipation Act, which declared the end to slavery. The execution thereof went step-by-step and around 1838 over 300,000 former slaves were now free citizens of Jamaica.

The consequences for the sugar plantations were huge, since the owners could not use free labour anymore. The next migration gulf was fed from Europe, mainly from Germany, Ireland and Scotland. Often it was forced emigration, fueled by the Great Famine in Ireland and the Highland Clearances in Scotland. Many people were shipped to the Caribbean as indentured servants, meaning one had to work for years to pay back the passage fee, before returning to Europe. In reality that hardly ever happened. The labourers did poorly in the heat, the work on the plantations was exhausting and many died as a result of these conditions. Those who survived looked for other work or moved away from the island, heading to North America. Labourers who emigrated from India and China dealt better with the climate. Africans also emigrated by the score, now out of their free will.

The plantations however, started to suffer since manual labour had become so expensive. On top of that Cuban sugar was sold far cheaper and Europe had discovered the sugar beet. Jamaica's decline in crops not only concerned sugar, but also tea, rice, tobacco and cotton.

The economy rapidly deteriorated and again the black, usually poor, community rose to protest, culminating in the Morant Bay Rebellion, led by another reverend. It turned into a true manifestation directed against British rule. The rebellion was suppressed, but it did lead to extensive reforms in law, government, police, health care, transport and education.

In 1872 the original capital of Spanish Town was swapped for Kingston, the latter having one of the largest natural harbours in the world. Around that time the banana export started to blossom. This fruit was grown by small-scale crofters as well at large plantations. The many banana boats that sailed from the harbour to faraway places would later inspire Harry Belafonte to compose the "Banana Boat Song".

Sugar cane crops were on the up again and the reforms in this particular industry led to a concentration of a few large sugar factories and rum distilleries. Currently one can find seven of them on the island.

Around 1900 a big exodus of Jamaicans to other places started. Large parties went to Panama and were employed in digging the eponymous canal. The northeast of the USA was a favourite place to go too, especially Boston, Philadelphia and New York. One could book affordable passage on the banana boats, which were sailing in those directions anyway.

The stagnating economy that would lead to a worldwide crisis in 1929 and the Second World War some ten years later, were overtures to a song of independence. The working class became more conscious of its latent political strength and began to organise itself in unions. 1938 had seen the founding of the democratic socialist People's National Party (PNP) by Norman Manly, to be followed by Sir Alexander Bustamante's Jamaica Labour Party (JLP) in 1943, the latter being the more liberal of the two.

In the mid 1950s the trek to Great Britain commenced. Between 1950 and 1960 an estimated 200,000 Jamaicans left their island and sailed to England. In the meantime the cry for independence grew louder. In 1934 Jamaica had received a restricted form of self-government and voting rights for the citizens. 1962 finally witnessed the much-desired state of independence and Bustamante was chosen the first Prime Minister of Jamaica. The JLP would reign for ten years with different PMs. In 1972 the PNP took over, with Norman Manley's son Michael at the helm.

PNP and JLP became mortal enemies and it is generally assumed that one time the CIA distributed weapons to promote the battle, honouring the motto "Divide and Conquer". The USA wasn't happy when the PNP rose to power, since Michael Manley chose a far more socialist course than the JLP. In doing so he openly courted neighbour Cuba. As the islands neared one another politically, it was not good for the Jamaican economy. After its declaration of independence, the USA basically considered Jamaica a profit rendering province. The American politicians did not like the Cuban love affair and economic sanctions were a logical consequence.

In 1980 Jamaica was in a poor position and the JLP regained power, led by PM Edward Seaga, who would play an important role in the popularisation of reggae, of which more in the eponymous chapter. Seaga set his sails direction USA and soon the economy started to blossom again, although the average Jamaican would only slightly notice the change of course.

Tourism became a main source of income, although the investments and profits came from and went into the pockets of foreign companies. The story mirrors the heydays of the sugar plantations, where absentee owners reaped the benefits and spent their fortunes in England. In other words, hardly anything changed for the local, often poor, black population.

PNP and JLP continued in battle, regularly fiercely and violently. Reggae icon and Jamaican hero Bob Marley would accidentally become involved in 1978, when he tried to reconcile Manley and Seaga at the *One Love Peace Concert* on April 22. They did shake hands on the podium, but not cordially. In 1989 the PNP took over, at first led again by Michael Manley. In 2007 the JLP won the elections and Bruce Golding became PM. The current Prime Minister is Portia Simpson-Miller.

Jamaica

Jamaica remains part of the Commonwealth of Nations, recently celebrating 50 years of independence. The official head of state is still Queen Elizabeth II. Deacon Sam Sharpe, who was hanged after the St James Revolt, has been declared a national hero. His name lives on in the big square at Montego Bay, where he lost his life in 1831.

***

In this snakepit of political unrest and upheaval, created when the Caribs tried to dine on the Arawaks, followed by the Spanish and British occupation, on the backs of slaves and indentured servants, the seed was sown for Jamaica's two most famous export goods – rum and reggae. I will tell about them in detail, but for a better understanding, first the history of sugar has to be explored.

TAB. XXVI.

Saccharum officinarum.   *Sugar Cane.*

SUGAR

Sugar

"Sugar island Cuba,
You lay there just for fun"
sang the members of the Dutch super group Focus in 1970,
on their debut album *In and Out of Focus*. Regardless of
the fact that the focus of this book is directed toward Jamaica and that the group were somewhat out of focus with
their lyrics – the word fun does not immediately spring
to my mind when mentioning Cuba – the latter island did
play an important role in growing sugar cane and manufacturing rum.

Christopher Columbus discovered Cuba in 1492, on
his first trip to the West. Originally he was Italian, born
in Geneva somewhere around October 1451. At the time
this city was an independent republic. However, he was
hired as an explorer by the king and queen of Spain, in
which country he was called Cristóbal Colón. Henceforth
his discoveries in the West Indies (currently known as the
Caribbean) were claimed as Spanish territory.

During his second trip, in 1494, he discovered Jamaica
and Hispaniola, the latter to be divided in two separate
parts some centuries later: Haiti and the Dominican Republic. On what island Columbus first introduced sugar
cane is not documented, but in importing the crop he did
kindle the flame and Jamaica would eventually grow into
one of the major players on the sugar cane field and the
distillation of rum. That growth cannot be credited to the

Spaniards, since the English kicked them out in 1655 and would rule the island until its independence in 1962.

Cuba remained in Spanish hands until 1898, when the Spanish-American war ended. In 1902 the island became independent. In the mid-1800s Great Britain shortly owned the capital Havana, but later exchanged that property with Spain for Florida. Those were the days.

The Caribbean witnessed a lot of fighting among the European powers between the 15th and 20th century. Many islands regularly changed hands, eventually ending up being owned by France, Spain or England. Almost everywhere sugar cane was planted, hence the term sugar islands.

One of the consequences of this triad is the fact that rum in general often is classified in French, Spanish and English styles. The Portuguese, having been present and active in the area for centuries, had eventually chosen the mainland of South America with their power base Brazil. They were the main player in the worldwide sugar industry, before the English took the stage.

Brazil has its own kind of rum, called cachaça. The Dutch, always keen on a piece of the pie, imported sugar from their colonies in the Far East and took possession of Surinam and some of the Antilles. Rum is manufactured in Surinam too. The Amsterdam company E&A Scheer was founded some 300 years ago and nowadays is one of the largest rum blenders and traders in the world. They buy and sell Caribbean rum as well as Indonesian arrack. The Dutch have always been more involved in the trade of sugar (and rum) than in growing the crop.

Sugar

The rise of sugar consumption in Europe did not start with the growing of sugar cane in the West Indies but earlier, with its import from the (Far) East. Columbus was an important transmitter who undoubtedly started the redistribution of power that sugar would hold for centuries, effectively relocating its base to the Caribbean. The Dutch were instrumental in the process, at the time owning huge possessions in both continents.

Before its introduction in the West Indies, sugar was mainly manufactured from sugar cane growing in the Dutch and Portuguese colonies of the Far East, a part of the world from where many spices were imported to Europe. At first the sweet crystals were seen as a spice and used accordingly. Sugar was also considered a medicine, supposedly relieving the few who could afford it from many ailments. At the time sugar was priceless.

Before Portugal crossed the Atlantic to explore the New World, the Portuguese had been experimenting with growing sugar cane on Madeira, the Azores and the Cape Verde islands. They used African slaves and they might have been the first nation to import slaves to the Caribbean and Brazil – a dubious honour. Spain did similar experiments on the Canary Islands, where rum is still made today. Some sources state that rum was invented on Gran Canaria. Knowledge and equipment would have been transported to the Caribbean from there. This is interesting fodder for discussion between the Spanish and the Portuguese (somewhat comparable with the one between Irish and Scots about the pedigree of whisky!).

Before the Caribbean took its role as the main supplier of cane sugar to Europe, the continent was mainly sugar-fed from said Spanish and Portuguese islands. In 1516 the Spanish king Charles I received the first sugar from his new Spanish profit province Hispaniola in the Caribbean.

The crop called sugar cane is far, far older. It officially belongs to the grasses and can grow up to 5 metres high within a year. Its history goes back, as far as we can trace, to approximately 6,000 years ago. New Guinea is often cited as the place of origin. The indigenous people used to chew on the young shoots, enjoying the sweet juice. It might have been considered a weed or herb.

Through cultivation, the growing of sugar cane steadily moved upward and eastward towards India, China and the Philippines. Not surprisingly so, since this crop performs excellently in (sub)tropical climates. Various sources claim that Indians have known how to manufacture sugar from sugar cane for millenia. The reeds were pressed and the resulting juice was heated and partly evaporated. After cooling down it would be curdled into a sticky clump of brown crystals, known as "sarkara" in Sanskrit. It is the root of our word "sugar".

A manuscript from ancient India called *Manasollana*, dated about 1,800 BC, contains a recipe for making sugar cane beer. Another manuscript from the same era refers to two alcoholic beverages made out of sugar. One is *sura*, made from sugar and rice, used to boost the morale of the soldiers. So when George Washington prescribed whiskey to his troops about 3,500 years later, he only repeated history. The other drink is called *soma*, an appetizer for the Indian aristocracy. The recipe and contents thereof remain unknown.

In the millennia that followed, the cultivation of sugar cane gained ground westward and during the reign of Alexander the Great (350 BC), the crystals extracted from sugar cane were described as "a kind of honey from a reed, without the assistance of bees." The Persian people introduced the crop to the east coast of the Mediterranean Sea where the Romans became acquainted with sugar. A tome from the year 95 AD mentions the word *sakchar* for "honey from reed." It is considered the first document showing there actually was a sugar trade with Europe.

The Arabs discovered sugar cane and its qualities when they invaded the Persian Empire in the 7th century. Now it was their turn to broaden the knowledge about sugar, even further to the west and north, with their conquest of what is now southern Spain.

Arabian documents from the 8th century describe distilling and it is not unthinkable that they might have distilled sugar cane juice, albeit on a modest scale. Anyhow, the Arabian alchemists knew how to refine raw sugars and developed a kind of syrup known as *Khurat al Milh*, the root of the contemporary word caramel.

In the 9th century people started to use sugar as a preservative. Honey was used before then but sucrose is much more effective, since it dehydrates and in doing so slows down growth of microorganisms. Even meat can be cured this way and kept for a considerable time. The tried and true method was coating and sealing foodstuffs with sugar crystals.

When the Knights Templar invaded Palestine around the 12th century and took sugar back home from their raids, Northern Europe learned about it. The amounts were minuscule, and sugar remained extremely expensive, mostly used at the European courts to impress guests.

The white crystals then might have been what diamonds are now, value wise. Sugar wasn't used as a sweetener but for decorative purposes to create so-called "subtleties". They were meant to entertain between courses during a lavish dinner and might resemble a complete castle with fighting knights, surrounded by forests and mountains. Our own birthday cake is a modest reminder of those days. Pharmacists sold perfumed sugar candy as medicine. Venice, Italy, became an important sugar refinery centre, where Cyprus and Sicily encouraged the growth of sugar cane.

Starting in the 14th century, small pieces of sugar candy were put in richly decorated small boxes and offered as a present to guests, mainly at the French court. Those boxes were called *drageoirs* and their contents *dragee.* The latter word still carries different meanings today, all stemming from the previous use of sugar through the ages:

A sugared nut, fruit or seed, often an almond,
a silver-coated candy bead to decorate pastries,
a sugar-coated medicine.

Sugar

In 1449 a mill with three rolls was invented on the island of Sicily and with it the cane pressing speed was multiplied. When Spain inherited this island they made good use of the technology. The southern part of Spain is the only part of the European continent where sugar cane can grow successfully, thanks to its climate: below 15 degrees Celsius (60° F), the shoots do not survive. Here the Moors had cultivated 30,000 hectare of sugar cane some centuries earlier. Rum is also produced in the area.

Early instructions for using sugar to prevent fermentation of fruits date from 1488. That is the origin of our modern tinned fruits (for example, peaches and pears) in syrup. Other documents tell us that English royalty enjoyed sugared fruits as early as the 15th century. Eventually that would evolve into jam and marmalade as we know it today.

Only when the Portuguese and English (Spaniards and French to a lesser extent), started to grow sugar cane in the Caribbean on a grand scale, sugar slowly became a commodity and found its way to the mass consumer market. The English fell in love with sugar – coining the expression "a sweet tooth" – and sugar consumption grew exponentially from 1750. The huge growth of use in England throughout the 18th century was stimulated by the import of tea. Originally the English had discovered the tea plant in China, but after adding India to the British Empire, they started to cultivate growing tea in the latter country.

One of the reasons why the English historically tend to drink far more tea than coffee might be that the former can absorb considerably more sugar than the latter and still be an agreeable drink. It is interesting to realise that the British collected the ingredients for their daily drink from India and the Caribbean. In doing so they united the Far East and the New World fluidly into a cup of tea on a green island in Western Europe!

Growing sugar cane and extracting sugar was very lucrative. Not for the islands as such, but for the owners of the sugar plantations and the mother country. By maintaining the mercantile system, in which colonies buy from and sell to the motherland, not much profit remained on the islands. All the money made went into the pockets of the absentee owners, who built huge mansions in their homeland to show off their incredible wealth. They were fond of keeping beautiful carriages, a habit which once elicited a much cited cry from king George II: "Sugar, sugar, always that sugar!" when he encountered a sugar baron driving a vehicle more splendid than his.

The goods of trade could only be transported by boats from the motherland, adding even more to the fortunes of the English ship owners. The "free employees", meaning imported African slaves and indentured servants, kept production very cheap. Their working and living circumstances were appalling, but nevertheless ignored by many an owner.

Only around 1850 mercantilism gradually disappeared in favour of the free market. In direct connection with this development was the abolition of slavery, begun in the late 1830s, although not all colonies simultaneously joined.

Now labour had to be paid. Prices were under pressure and sugar became affordable for the masses.

In 1650 sugar had been a rarity in Western Europe. In 1750 its status as "white gold" had changed to a luxury good and from 1850 it was considered a vital necessity. Processing of sugar in (pre)prepared food, not only for the taste but also for preservation, added to the serious growth in consumption.

Was there any alternative to sugar cane? Sure. Around 1600 the Frenchman Olivier de Serres had discovered sugar crystals in beetroot. It would take one and a half centuries before German Andreas Margraff succeeded in extracting its juices and crystallize the liquid, albeit of no commercial use in 1747.

As so often in history, necessity is the mother of invention. After the French Revolution and during the Napoleonic Wars, approximately between 1800 and 1815, the British blockaded the import of sugar to the European mainland, resulting in a shortage. Another German, Franz Carl Achard, invented a method to enhance the level of sugar in the beetroot, by applying selective growth. The sugar beet was born. It could grow in a moderate climate, much to the advantage of Western Europe.

When the Napoleonic Wars were over, the cultivation of sugar beets temporarily declined and sugar cane became an affordable alternative for a while. This was ended by the abolition of slavery and the sugar beet continued its rise in importance during the next century.

In 1968 the European Community (EC) started to interfere, in an attempt to regulate the sugar market. The EC increased the import tax on sugar manufactured outside Europe, among other regulations. Since 2006 steps toward deregulation have been taken by its successor the EU, ultimately resulting in unlimited imports. But...the sugar beet is not suitable for making palatable rum. That's why I will not further elaborate on its history. So let's turn to the sugar cane fields and the production of sugar, molasses and rum. I will use three plantations on Jamaica to help illustrate the process.

***

Jamaicans often use the word farm or factory instead of plantation. Once the island was dotted with them, but during consecutive slave revolts many were burnt and destroyed. Some remarkably survived, as is the case with Worthy Park and Appleton Estate. They still grow sugar cane. Others found a new lease of life as a stand alone eco-tourism attraction, such as Good Hope Plantation, where growing sugar cane and citrus fruits are not core activities anymore.

Good Hope's history is a fascinating one and can be traced back to 1742, when Colonel Thomas Williams received 400 hectares of Crown Estate from King George II. Two years later he built his first mansion on the estate. Its ruins can still be seen. The current main house was erected in 1775 for his son's bride, who sadly died shortly thereafter from yellow fever. She is buried near the entrance to the living room.

The young widower soon ran into debt and was forced to sell the estate in 1767 to his neighbour John Tharp, who at 23 showed a real talent for business. He owned another estate, Potosi, acquired via marrying a certain Elizabeth Partridge. It conveniently bordered Good Hope. The Tharp family would considerably enhance their lands and turn both estates into a very profitable sugar cane plantation.

Contrary to many other plantation owners who chose to reside in England, appointing a manager and hiring a lawyer to take care of their business, John Tharp preferred to stay on the island and personally manage his business affairs. He lived the larger part of his life on Jamaica, which seriously contributed to the good fortune of Good Hope.

Tharp not only was prolific as a sugar baron, but also as a father. With his wife he begot four sons and a daughter. Before he was married he had fathered a son with a slave woman. The boy answered to the name John Harewood and was certainly not neglected. Eventually he was appointed manager of all his father's possessions.

Tharp was an enlightened aristocrat and built John a house, a hospital for the slaves and various other annexes. Slowly but steadily he acquired more property. When he died in 1804, his estate encompassed nearly the entire province of Trelawney, from the mountains in the south to the sea in the north; from Chippenham Park in the east to Westmoreland in the west. He also owned a few houses in the nearby town of Falmouth, a 2,400-hectare estate in England and a house in London.

This illustrates how incredibly rich the English sugar barons were at the beginning of the 19th century. Tharp's will stipulated that at least 3,000 slaves should be kept on the premises in order to secure efficient production. The time period considered, he had been a good caretaker, which paid off after his demise – Good Hope was protected by its slaves and thus spared during the great slave revolt of 1832.

1867 witnessed the end of the Tharp era on Good Hope. The new owner, a Mr Coy from Falmouth, decided to remove all iron and mahogany on the estate, sell it and concentrated on profitably running the sugar plantation. This cannot be said about the next owner, Alexander Oppenheimer, a retired sea captain. He acquired the estate in 1898 but brought it to the edge of ruin. The story goes he spent his time and money on rum and women. The plantation slowly overgrew with weeds and nature took control.

That period ended with the arrival of an American banker on the island, in 1912. He was looking for antique furniture and locals suggested he should visit Good Hope. It took some time to find the place, overgrown as it was, and the welcome wasn't of the cordial kind. Oppenheim chased him off the premises with a loaded gun. On his way back the banker, named Thompson, stopped in Falmouth for a drink, probably to calm his nerves. As it happens the captain walked in but the outcome would seriously differ from their first meeting. When they parted company, Good Hope had a new owner.

Thompson immediately started renovating the place.

Not only were the buildings restored to their former splendour, but the soil was also cultivated anew, this time for growing coconut palms. He also opened the hunt for stray cattle and wild hogs, which had taken possession of the lands in the previous decade.

Thompson's son Howard was appointed manager and from 1933 visitors could pay for a visit to Good Hope and enjoy themselves on the surrounding grounds. In the 20 years to come the estate became famous with adventurers as well as royalty. Princess Alice (1901-2004), aunt to Queen Elizabeth II, often stayed at the house. She loved visiting Jamaica, and was even honored with the position as First Chancellor of the University of the West Indies.

When Irishman Patrick Tenison took over Good Hope in 1950, the former sugar plantation was known as an excellent high quality lodging for the rich and (in)famous. With his wife Fran he ran the hotel/annex guesthouse until 1970, when the political situation in Jamaica turned rather unstable and tourism declined. Tenison locally gained the nickname Mr Clock, due to the fact that one of his arms was not fully-grown. Jamaicans love nicknames, something I had the pleasure of experiencing myself during our stay in a family owned hotel in the hills northwest of Good Hope. My light skin and long, grey hair fascinated the beautiful four-year-old daughter of the proprietor. Upon our arrival she greeted me with "Hello, Mr Polar Bear" and continued to call me that for the length of our stay.

In 1989 Tenison decided to sell Good Hope and Covey Estate, which he owned as well, to a consortium of inves-

tors, lead by local businessman Tony Hart, 7th generation Jamaican of English descent. Hart played an important role in the development of Jamaican music, since he was the first to own and exploit a record press on the island. It comes as no surprise that his good friend and neighbour is contemporary and record company owner Chris Blackwell, founder of Island Records.

For the second time during its existence Good Hope was not in Good Shape. Tenison had acquired much acreage, but did not have enough cash to maintain the property appropriately. Nature again had reclaimed what previously had been cultivated. The new owners, like Thompson, thoroughly renovated the place and currently various crops are grown on a small scale, mainly papaya, ackee and some sugar cane.

Tony Hart bought out his co-investors and handed Good Hope over to his son Blaise, who intends to expand the current ecotourism and outdoor attractions in their historical setting. Quad bikes, horseback, zipline or a guided walking tour are all ways to appreciate and enjoy this beautiful location. One can tour the restored plantation home and have lunch on the property, or visit the pottery on site. The old water mill is partly restored and one of the annexes houses a restaurant cum souvenir shop. Rum was never made commercially in this place but one can taste and buy some.

***

That is not the case with Worthy Park Estate, two hours by car to the east, more or less in the geographical centre of Jamaica.

As a reward for chasing away the Spaniards in 1655, Sir Charles Price received a parcel of Jamaica, 340 hectares in size and in 1670 he registered his possession as Worthy Park. Around 1710 the cultivation of sugar cane and the production of sugar commenced, which has not stopped since. The history of the estate is extremely well documented. That's why we know for certain that rum production started in 1741. Since 1783 the owners had noted down detailed production figures. The Price family invested part of the proceeds in improving the roads surrounding the plantation.

A peak in production was reached in 1812, with 705 hogsheads of sugar and 350 puncheons of rum, the equivalent of 111,300 litres. Then production slowly decreased and in 1838 – the year marking abolition of slavery in Jamaica – the output was a meagre 140 hogsheads. From 1845 onward indentured servants from India were sent as substitutes for the former slaves, a practise that would end in 1917. By that time Worthy Park had changed hands. In June 1863 the company was sold by the Encumbered Estate Commission (indicating that things had gone seriously wrong) to the Earl of Shrewsbury and Talbot. It ended the Price era.

The new owner enlarged the plantation in two stages between 1874 and 1881 to 4,000 hectares. Then, in 1889, Worthy Park was sold again, this time to Mr J.B. Calder,

who kept a herd of over 800 cows as well as introducing cacao and bananas on the plantation.

In 1918 the company with all its grounds was acquired by Frederick Clarke, who reorganised and considerably enlarged the plantation until his demise in 1932. His son Clement took charge and again expanded, this time with cultivating citrus fruit. Houses and a sports field were erected on the estate, especially for the employees.

In the early 1960s rum production came to a grinding halt, caused by an agreement with the Spirits Pool Association (the Jamaican equivalent of the Scotch Whisky Association) to reduce distilling Jamaican rum, in order to get rid of the overproduction created after the Second World War.

1970 was Worthy Park's tri-centennial for which occasion the Clarke Family donated 1200 hectares of land to the Jamaican government, earmarked for erecting affordable housing. To date this has not happened (!) To add to the festivities a book about the estate was published. In the following decades the estate managed to survive crop disease, a large fire and hurricane Gilbert, which devastated large parts of Jamaica in 1988. A mere five years later, in 1993, sugar production was fully up and running again, with an annual output of 241,301 tons. When in 1994 the Tristeza virus threatens the citrus fruit, the management decided to dedicate that 365 hectares solely to sugar cane again.

The current director of Worthy Park is great-grandson Gordon C. Clarke. In 2013 he is responsible for a company that has been growing sugar cane and producing sugar uninterruptedly for 342 years. As of 2004 he is a distillery manager too, since he decided to restart the production of rum, albeit on a modest scale. Before taking over the management of Worthy Park, he worked for Wray & Nephew (W&N), the largest sugar and rum producer of Jamaica. Worthy Park is not open to visitors.

***

This brings us automatically to Appleton Estate, part of W&N. Here, in the Nassau Valley of St Elizabeth parish, sugar cane has been growing for centuries. In 1749 rum distilling commenced, with success, as evidenced that it has continued for over 263 years.

Anyone who wants to see how sugar was produced in early times and what changes have occurred over time, will enjoy a visit to Appleton. For more than 25 years special tours have been conducted that take the visitor through three centuries of sugar production, after which the rum distillery is viewed. Then, to top it off, a tutored tasting of rum ends a worthwhile visit. But before we are to engage in rum, let's have a closer look at growing sugar cane and harvesting sugar from the crop.

Sugar cane usually grows a minimum of 10 months up to two years – depending on the species, the climate and the condition of the soil – before it can be harvested.

At Appleton it takes one year. Harvesting is done from January until May, both mechanically and manually, using machetes. Before man and machine enter the fields,

sections are burnt with controlled fire, mainly in the relative cool of the evening, to prevent overheating. The sugar cane is not damaged, due to its high water content, but the burning kills off pests and microorganisms, removes undergrowth and strips the stalk of "trash" – tops and leaves. After burning a field, the sugar cane has to be harvested within 24 hours. If it takes longer, the amount of sugar in the cane decreases dramatically.

Sugar cane grows back. New shoots are called *rattoons*. Every four to five years – again depending on local circumstances – a field is newly sown.

Mature and harvested sugar cane needs to be pressed. In the 17th century this was manual labour and an estimated 65-70% of the juice present in the cane could be gained. Then it would be boiled in a series of copper kettles. By cooling the hot liquid with water in a porous limestone pot, brown crystals appeared, together with a by-product, molasses. The filtered water was rich in calcium and supposedly healthy for pregnant women. The Jamaican soil is rich with limestone and Spanish settlers used such pots four centuries ago. A specimen is on display at Appleton's.

The industrial revolution did not skip the island and in the second half of the 18th century, mills were built that could be operated by man and/or animal. Appleton still has a model with a donkey providing the energy. Paz, as Appleton's visitor centre donkey is called, is attached to a vintage Chattanooga Cane Mill around which he walks in a circle. His motion turns the rollers that squeeze liquid out of the cane that is hand-fed through the mill. The juice is collected in a wooden vat. The reward for the animal is the processed piece of cane. Not far from this mill you can press your own cane juice, if you are willing to take your turn at a smaller mill. The Famous Spouse and I decided to do that and can tell from experience it is heavy duty, especially when the sun burns with temperatures above 30 degrees Celsius (85° F). The juice is refreshing and sweet, having an herbal finish.

Today things are quite a bit more advanced by further mechanisation of the process. As soon as the sugar cane is transported from the plantation to the sugar factory, the reeds are cleaned, cut in pieces and milled. The cane itself consists of 75% water, 10-16% sugar and 10-16% fibres.

Compared with the 17th century, one can now gain 25% more juice from the cane. The collected liquid is boiled under pressure after which a sticky substance emerges, containing 30% sugar. The sticky syrup is cleared and mixed with sugar crystals that form the base on which the dissolved sugar in the liquid can grow new crystals. The mix is repeatedly brought to a boiling point and cooled until the crystals have the desired size.

During cooling the crystals continue to grow. After cooling, the mass enters an industrial centrifuge that separates the liquid from the crystals. The resulting sugar is called first grade sugar and its by-product first grade molasses. The latter is still rich in sugars and will be cooked and centrifuged again, resulting in second grade sugar and second grade molasses. The first and second grade sugar is then sold to the world market, its colour brown.

By way of refining, the colour will get whiter and the structure of the sugar finer. Certain nutrients will be lost in the process. Refining sugar takes place primarily in North America and Europe, but also in the Middle and Far East. In days gone by the bulk of sugar was refined and stored in English port cities, where the Caribbean raw sugar would arrive. Nearly all the old sugar warehouses and factories have been demolished but in Bristol one can still find two beautifully repurposed warehouses. One is converted into office and apartment space; the other now serves as a boutique hotel with many original details from its former use. The second grade molasses is heated and centrifuged again. The resulting low-grade sugar will be used in the next round to propagate the growth of new sugar crystals. The fibres remaining after pressing are also called bagasse. They are put to use for the manufacture of press-board furniture and for heating industrial boilers in the sugar factory. The heat is evenly spread over the boilers via vents. This invention is called "The Jamaican Train". The molasses that remains after the last heating and centrifuging cycle is used to make...rum!

What is the average harvest of one hectare sugar cane, grown in the Caribbean? Well, to begin we are looking at 5.6 tonnes of first grade sugar. Then there is 13.3 tons of wet bagasse (50% solid, 50% liquid), which equates to 2.4 tonnes of fuel oil. The third and last component is approximately 1.5 tonnes of molasses from which no consumable sugar can be extracted. In some way the process may be compared to the making of whisky, whereby also virtually nothing is wasted and by-products are re-used in the next cycle or for other purposes.

CALYPSO
very old
Jamaica-Rum
ALC. 38 %
PRODUCE OF JAMAICA
BOTTLED IN HOLLAND BY B.A.M. AMSTERDAM
REG. TRADE-MARK.

RUM

Rum

The Latin name for sugar cane is *Saccharum officinarum*. It is tempting to see the etymology of the word rum herein, but that would be historically unjust. The first time rum was used as a noun in a document was in 1661, and Linnaeus first used the official naming of this plant in 1753. Apart from that there are many Latin words ending in (r)um. The early document was a rum order placed by the Governor of Jamaica, the island having changed hands between the Spanish and English six years earlier.

It is generally assumed that the word itself was derived from another document from Barbados, dated 1651, in which can be read: "The chief fuddling they make in the island is Rum-bullion, alias Kill-Divil, and this is made of sugar canes distilled, a hot, hellish, and terrible liquor." The word rumbullion died in the English language, possibly being abbreviated to rum.

The English treated the Gaelic *uisge beatha* in a similar matter, bastardising the word to "whisky". The quote above feeds the assumption that Barbados might have been the first rum producer in history, added to which is the fact that the English had taken Barbados earlier than Jamaica. The former island is located far more to the east and is, contrary to most Caribbean islands, very flat and therefore relatively easy to cultivate.

It remains a question when and where the drink showed up for the first time. Some sources point to a similar beverage that was produced in Brazil around 1620. That would put the Portuguese on the first spot as the oldest makers of rum. But, rum is called cachaça in Brazil and made slightly differently than all Caribbean rum, with the exception of the French variety. All in all there is no certainty in what year and what country the name and the drink first appeared.

The order of a high-ranking English government official is not the only reason why Jamaica has such a strong connection with rum. In 1655 when Admiral Penn conquered Jamaica, he ordered that his crew should have a ration of rum, which would later be known as the "tot". Before his command, the English navy mainly drank beer. In 1590 the ration of beer per head was one gallon*, to be divided equally during the different meals on board. Mind you, we're talking about 4.5 litres of beer per day per person!

In the early days rum was a cheap, strong tasting liquor made from the by-product molasses that remains after sugar juice had been extracted from the cane and boiled into crystals. Rum was given to the slaves to keep them sedated. Brandy was the choice of drink among English naval officers, notwithstanding Penn's generous 1655 decision. Due to rum's lack of quality, this was understanda-

---

In 1824 the British, or Imperial gallon, was standardized to 4.54 litres. The USA created its own standard in 1899, the US gallon, or 3.78 litres. In the history before 1899 I used the British standard. This also applies to pints and quarts, which differ in volume in both countries.

ble. Only when it considerably improved, was rum actually prescribed, as can be read in a letter from Samuel Pepys. As a secretary to the Navy he wrote: "Approval given to Mr Waterhouse to supply King James's ships at Jamaica with Rumm instead of Brandy (sic)". The letter contained a caveat. The experiment should be monitored closely and within two years reports should present the good or ill effects of the trial on seamen's health – and whether they were satisfied with the substitution. It's not difficult to guess the outcome…

From 1731 onward every member of the Royal Navy received half a pint of rum per day, about 0.3 litre, usually taken in one session. That was a bit too much of the good stuff and accidents occurred regularly. Admiral Vernon is credited with putting a halt to that custom. He had been in the Caribbean since 1708, beating the hell out of the Spaniards. Now Vernon ordered that the rum should be diluted with a quart of water (approximately 1 litre). He also added "those who behave as a good husband should be given extra lime juice and sugar". This order, given on August 21, 1740, is noted down as Captain's Order Number 349. Not long after it had taken effect, Vernon's crew looked much healthier than other seafaring men. In 1747 the British naval doctor James Lind made the connection and in doing so became the discoverer of a means to end scurvy – vitamin C in citrus fruit. The word "grog", a punch containing rum and fruits, is derived from the habit installed by Vernon. The admiral's nickname was "Old Grog", in itself a derivation of his waterproof coat – a so-called grogram.

In roughly 70 years rum's popularity had risen enormously. In 1698 only 207 gallons of rum were imported by England, but in 1765 the amount had seen a rise of two million gallons, the equivalent of more than nine million litres (somewhat near the amount annually produced by a Scottish single malt whisky distillery the likes of Glenfiddich). In 1781 Thomas Trotter, a poet who would remain virtually unknown, had written a few lines referring to Vernon's action and the consequences:

> *...A mighty bowl on deck he drew,*
> *and filled it to the brink;*
> *Such drank the Burford's gallant crew,*
> *And such the gods shall drink.*
> *The sacred robe which Vernon wore,*
> *Was drenched within the same;*
> *And hence his virtues guard our shore,*
> *And Grog derives its name.*

The English had turned rum into a national drink and they wanted the world to know it. Admiral Nelson, who served in the Caribbean before he was mortally wounded in 1805 during the battle of Trafalgar, supposedly had said on more than one occasion, that, should he die in battle, his body had to be shipped to England in a cask full of rum. In those days it was not unusual to use rum as an embalming fluid, owing to lack of a refrigerator or freezer compartment on board. Nelsons body indeed was shipped in a cask with a strong alcoholic beverage. A legend claims his mourning crew would regularly take sips from the cask during the voyage home. From this event rum has gained one of its many nicknames: Nelson's Blood.

In reality it was a cask of Spanish brandy, mixed with camphor and myrrh. During the journey the cask was tied to the main mast and guarded meticulously. The Spaniards called their brandy *aguardiente* and sugar cane was grown in the south of Spain. Since Nelson's body was shipped to England from Gibraltar, it might have contained a kind of rum indeed.

That story shows the history of rum is drenched in myths and legends, somewhat comparable with the history of whisky. Before the latter drink started its world-wide conquest, rum was the world drink par excellence. This was partly due to the immense British Empire – upon which the sun never set. That description has been credited to King Charles I of Spain, who once had a similar tract of land.

Everywhere in the world the British Navy appeared on the shores and in its wake, rum, lots of rum. Where the British founded colonies, rum still is produced; not only in Jamaica and other Caribbean islands, but also in India and Australia.

Rum was generously used as a bartering tool, for instance on the African west coast to buy slaves and by pirates who had embraced rum and bought meat with it, among other goods. Originally they did not use rum for barter. When rum quality still left much to be desired, they preferred cognac, stolen from French ships. Many pirates, among whom the aforementioned Henry Morgan, were villains paid by the English to fight with the French and Spaniards, with whose countries England had been at war almost continuously. Morgan lived to become governor of Jamaica, but that cannot be said about all his former cronies. In 1720 the British Navy captured John Rackham after he and his crew had been indulging in a huge amount of looted rum. They were too drunk to fight and ended on the gallows. Blackbeard was known for intimidating his opponents by drinking burning rum, honouring his nickname.

Another famous, true story that was successfully turned into a book and much later into a movie, in which rum played an important role, is *The Mutiny on the Bounty*. On April 28, 1789 Captain Bligh was put in a seven metre long sloop, together with 18 loyal crewmembers, near Tahiti. The revolting crew appeared to have given up the hard sea life, in favour of the beautiful and charming Tahitian ladies. Bligh, who was taught by captain Cook, managed to navigate to Timor in the Indonesian archipelago within 47 days. At the time it belonged to the Dutch East Indies. During the gruesome voyage only one man had died in hand combat at the island Tofua, where Bligh had tried to get provisions in vain. At sea he had kept his remaining crew alive and motivated by daily portions of rum.

One year after the mutiny, Bligh was court marshalled but found not guilty and his honour was restored. He received an assignment to transport breadfruit from Tahiti to the British Caribbean. In Jamaica he not only encountered rum but also an indigenous fruit called ackee. He took a sample back to England and presented it to the Royal Society, who credited him by giving it a scientific name. Since then the ackee is officially known as *Blighia sapida*. The captain's star was on the rise again and he served under Nelson during the battle of Copenhagen in 1801. Later the admiral would praise his contribution to the victory.

A few years later Bligh was rewarded with the post of Governor of New South Wales, in Australia. He arrived in August 1806 and found massive corruption among the population. This was no wonder since England had been using Australia extensively as a penal colony for a century or so. Villains, crooks and thieves were simply transported to down under.

Corruption had spread to and infected civil servants and officers of the British army. Bligh did not appreciate that. He used the smuggling of rum as a stick to beat the dog, but he thrashed the wrong backs and made many enemies among the landed gentry, such as gentleman farmer John MacArthur and Thomas Jamison, surgeon general of the colony. The offices of the New South Wales Corps were on their side and in 1808 the conflict grew into what became known in history books as the Rum Rebellion.

This time Bligh was not ditched as a captain but as a governor and again rum was at the core of his problems. At first Major George Johnston put him in prison, but eventually he was allowed to return to England, where he was court marshalled for the second time in his life,

now in May 1810. Again he was rehabilitated and Johnston convicted. Bligh was promoted Rear Admiral, to be
followed with a promotion to Vice Admiral of the Blue in
1814, but did not play an important role anymore. Rum
did and still does, since Australia continued to make rum.
One of the best-known brands down under is Bundaberg.
An Australian punk-folk band named itself Rum Rebellion.
Well, it's not reggae but you might want to sample "Drink
with the Devil (Pick your Poison)": http://www.youtube.
com/watch?v=wzcOv300_pk.

On January 1, 1851 the amount of rum for the Navy's
tot was reduced to 1/8 pint. It would take more than 120
years before the Royal Navy banned rum entirely. On the
31st of July in the year 1970 this ancient ritual was officially ended and that day became known as "Black Tot
Day". Seamen did receive a small financial compensation
in place of their tot.

The American Navy had banned rum in 1862. At that
point in time rum, having been the tipple of choice, was on
a downhill slide in America. This was caused by different
factors. First there were the opponents of slavery. Antho-
ny Benezet, a well-known abolitionist from Philadelphia,
had published a pamphlet in 1767, in which he joined rum
and slavery at the hip. A bit short-sighted perhaps, but he
did have a point to prove. The sugar cane plantations had
grown into successful businesses by harvesting sugar and
producing rum on the backs of the slaves. Rum was also
used to subdue them.

Around 1790 whiskey had silently taken a 30% market

share in the USA as far as distilled spirits were concerned and that growth would continue well into the 19th century, when Scottish and Irish immigrants became more influential in distilling. Most whiskey was made in Kentucky and Tennessee, areas where sugar cane could not grow. The distance to any port made the import of molasses prohibitive to those distilleries.

What also contributed was the fact that rum and molasses were taxed far heavier than whiskey and grains. The rum made in New England wasn't as tasty as its Caribbean counterpart and mainly taken for the effect of the alcohol. American whiskey simply tasted better and was much cheaper than North American rum. Even President Washington started to distil at his Mount Vernon Estate, at the turn of the century, with the help of a Scottish distiller.

During the Civil War both sides were amply supplied with whiskey, to boost the morale and as an antiseptic for the wounded, especially when limbs had to be amputated. President Abraham Lincoln once said about his successful general Ulysses Grant: "Tell me what brand of whiskey that Grant drinks. I would like to send a barrel of it to my other generals." The American Navy not only banned their rum tot, but also made a serious attempt to block all import of Caribbean rum in favour of the more patriotic whiskey.

When the war was over, a war not aimed at abolition of slavery alone, but also an economic battle between the north and the south, the consumption of rum was even more suppressed. The association with slavery was a logical one and the nation did not want to be reminded about that black page in its history. Literally and figuratively speaking rum had gone dark. The economic blockades were banished but the south, once thriving and affluent, lay in ruins and not much money could be spent on luxuries like imported, distilled drinks. Hence, a large and important consumer market had gone down the drain.

In the mean time the Christian Temperance Movement had gained ground and become more influential in political circles. The state of Maine was the first to go dry, ordered in 1851 by Major Neal Dow. His decree resulted in the Portland Rum Riot, during which skirmish one man was killed and seven injured. It was a temporary setback for the Movement and the ban on alcohol was lifted in 1856. However, it was a sign of the times. The devil disguised as rum was cast out by increasing numbers of people.

Rum became a synonym for all strong alcoholic beverages and those who supported abstention showed themselves very creative in donning new expressions with the word rum in it. Rumrunners were liquor smugglers; a search by Customs was called rummaging, at the time meaning "to search closely (the hold of a ship), especially by moving things about".

Well, one state after the other went dry, eventually culminating in National Prohibition on January 19, 1920. The Scots now would start to build an important trade position in the Americas by delivering huge amounts of whisky to Canada and the Bahamas, from where "merchants" smuggled goods into the USA. The Scots kept their hands clean, since their customers were technically outside America.

When Repeal came on December 5, 1933, the USA was legally flooded with Scotch and the drink was embraced enthusiastically. Not only rum but also bourbon became a bottom shelf product. The distilling industry as a whole had fallen apart and needed to be virtually rebuilt from scratch. The whiskey men among them succeeded better than the rum distillers from New England.

Just after the Noble Experiment, there was not much indigenous alcohol at hand in the USA. Whisky was imported from Europe and rum from the Caribbean. The latter was now often used as an ingredient in a cocktail and not drunk neat anymore. This development was boosted by the habits of Ernest Hemingway, who enjoyed a Mojito and made a lot of noise about that. For whom the bell tolls, so to speak.

A bartender in Los Angeles opened a cocktail bar in a Polynesian style – the tiki bar– and named his joint Don the Beachcomber. The bar was in instant hit with the Hollywood crowd. Entrepreneur Vic Bergeron copied the model in San Francisco under the name Trader Vic. He presented his own version of a rum cocktail, The Mai Tai, meaning "good" in Tahitian. Captain Bligh would turn in his grave if he knew. Both bars were the prototypes of the current cocktail bars. Rum was now concealed in other drinks.

During the Second World War most distilleries turned to producing industrial alcohol for the weapons industry. This had an ill effect on rum production. During the 1960s and 1970s a new trend emerged: the colourless and tasteless cocktail mixer called vodka. The whisky distillers in Scotland would seriously feel that. Around 1980 a true whisky lake was created, due to years of overproduction, notwithstanding that the distillers knew the bland, popular vodka was eating up their market share. At the end of the 1980s, the consumer started to look for tastier drinks again. Bourbon, blended whisky and single malts showed an upsurge. In their slipstream rum emerged, especially the darker varieties with lots of body and taste.

Today rum has found an honourable place between old cognacs and vintage single malts. It is no longer only relegated to a mixed drink so popular in the first half of the 20th century. Now one can often find mature rum at the liquor store: 20 and even 30-year-old rum is not an exception any longer.

It seems all countries around the world want to participate in rum's comeback. In my country of birth, the Netherlands, drinks specialist Jan Beek created two rums for the domestic market only. With the Amsterdam based rum blender E&A Scheer he created the Ultimatum Infinitum 12 and the Ultimatum Summum 25. Jan used no less than twelve rums from eight different distilleries, located in Jamaica, Barbados, Trinidad and Guyana. The rums used are from different vintages and the older expressions have been maturing in a so-called Solera-system, as has been used in the sherry industry for ages. The Infinitum is light and fresh, the Summum more heavily bodied with layers of flavour. Taste is as personal as it gets, but I do enjoy them and they are worth a special mention.

Cooking with rum has become popular as well. The Home Cooking website of the *New York Times* dedicates an entire section to rum recipes (see homecooking.about.com/library/archive/blrum.htm). By the way, rum in the kitchen is definitely not a new fad. For decades rum has been generously used, in flambéing, marinating and infusion. As a young boy I would eat my mother's home baked cake with raisins soaked in rum. As an 8-year-old I managed to get tipsy on a delicacy called "rumbonen", a kind of rum-filled chocolate bonbon. But, let's not digress. It's time to take a look at how rum is actually made.

According to some, it is a waste product of sugar harvesting, according to others, a by-product. For the taste it doesn't matter what you call it. How rum is made and where, does have serious consequences. Not every country uses the same specifications and this may lead to confusion among the consumers. Scotch has to be produced, matured and bottled in Scotland; Bordeaux wine in the French region of Bordeaux and bourbon is an indigenous product of the USA. Rum does not acknowledge such a geographic distinction. It is also written differently in various countries: ron, rom, rhum, rum, arrack, cachaça - whereas the "barley wine" is only written as whisky or whiskey. Funnily enough one of the Scottish Hebrides, to the west of the mainland, is called Rum, sometimes written as Rhum. As far as my knowledge goes, there is no rum distillery to be found on the tiny island.

The land of production defines how rum must be made. Consequently there are many definitions. I will limit myself to those used by the USA and the European Union. According to the Bureau of Alcohol, Tobacco, Firearms and Explosives (ATF) rum is: "Spirits distilled from the fermented juice of sugar cane, sugar cane syrup, sugar cane molasses or other sugar cane by-products at less than 95% alcohol by volume (190 proof) having the taste, aroma and characteristics generally attributed to rum and bottled at not less than 40% alcohol by volume (80 proof), including mixtures of such distillates." Really, in one sentence!

The EU description is similar: "A strong alcoholic liquor solely produced through alcoholic fermentation and distillation, either from molasses of syrup produced during the harvesting of sugar cane sugar or its juice and distilled below 96% ABV, with the distillate containing the noticeable specific organoleptic characteristics of rum."

Be my guest! I prefer to savour a glass instead of reading the stuff above. It is remarkable however that the Europeans smuggle an extra 1% of alcohol by volume into the distillate. Bottled rum in Europe has to have a minimum of 37.5% ABV to be legally called rum.

The most important ingredient is the base material. And everywhere around the world, or so it should be, that base is sugar cane. Nearly every distiller in the Caribbean produces rum from molasses, except the French. They call their beverage *rhum agricole* and distil from the fermented cane juice, instead of the molasses. It is a production method somewhat similar to the making of cachaça in Brazil, once introduced by the Portuguese. Sugar cane can also be used to make vodka, but let us concentrate on rum.

Most often, rum's base is molasses, created during the harvesting of sugar from the sugar cane, as can be read in the chapter about sugar. The composition of molasses is important for the eventual taste of the rum produced. Tests have shown that molasses from sugar beets is unsuitable. If distilled it is not very tasty. Molasses from sugar cane produces the best rum when its viscosity is low, its nitrogen and sugar contents high, and its ash and sulphur contents low.

In the early days, molasses had to be immediately processed to prevent spontaneous fermentation. The discovery that molasses could be concentrated and kept longer meant it could be transported over long distances before use. New England, at the time still a colony of Great Britain, profited and in Boston, among other places, a large rum industry came into being. Plenty of rum made there found its way to the motherland via English ships and to West Africa, as a bartering tool to fetch new slaves, who in their turn were set to work at the Caribbean plantations, harvesting the sugar cane. The latter was processed into sugar and molasses, of which part would be transported to New England. Again this is a representative example of the Mercantile Triangle, which in reality did not consist of one but various trade triangles.

When molasses is diluted with water and yeast added, the result is a low-alcohol fluid (about 8% ABV), which, as in the whisky industry, is called wash. One rum distillery prefers to buy yeast from a central plant, where another, for example Appleton or Worthy Park, use proprietary

OW WINE →

POT STILL

This is a distillation of whisky from fermented wort. The pot still is heated and the alcohol vapour rises and passes through the cooling system.

yeast strains, kept alive at the distillery. During fermentation an important part of the eventual flavours is created. Long fermentation cycles produce so-called high esters that do not appear when yeasting is done in shorter cycles. The next step is distillation. Pot stills are used at Worthy Park while Appleton has a combination of pot and column stills. This will also seriously influence the taste of the end product.

Distillation in a pot still takes five to six hours and happens in three steps. In fact, it is triple distillation in three connected stills. The first step takes place in the pot still itself, usually indirectly heated (in the old days open fires were used, but that practice was abandoned due to safety regulations and efficiency measures). The alcohol vaporises and descends into the low wines retort, bubbling through a liquid containing approximately 30% ABV. The vapours are re-heated and show up in the high wines retort with about 60% ABV. The process is repeated and the vapours end up in the condenser, carrying up to 85% ABV. As soon as the alcohol content of the liquid reaches a certain lower level, the remaining liquid is distilled and condensed. These "feints" are collected separately and used in a next round.

With single malt whisky, a spirit safe is used to divide the foreshots, middle cut and feints, to prevent methanol and fusel oils from getting in the eventual whisky. With rum distilling that is not necessary due to the low amount of pectins in the molasses, resulting in virtually no methanol in the distilled spirit.

Column still distillation is carried out in a Coffey still, used in Scotland and Ireland for distilling grain alcohol. This installation, designed in 1831 by Aeneas Coffey, is still in use in the industry. It consists of two tall, inter-connected columns – the analyser and the rectifier – both divided into subsections by means of perforated plates. The wash enters the rectifier via a pipe (usually copper, but not always), at the bottom. From there another pipe takes the wash to the top of the analyser where the wash is poured out over the topmost plate. The liquid starts to trickle down through the compartments. At the same time steam is fed into the bottom of the analyser. When ascending through the perforated plates it meets and heats the wash, stripping the latter from its alcohol.

The vapours are sent via another pipe to the bottom of the rectifier and will ascend anew. Since different alcohols fractionize at different temperatures, the spirit separates itself in various parts, of which the heavier alcohols condense back into liquid form and lay on top of the plates. Hence, only the lighter alcohols can reach the top of the column, hitting a massive plate, ending up in a condenser and collected afterwards.

The alcohol resulting from these columns is "cleaner" than pot still alcohol but certainly not neutral. The master distiller can tweak the installation and create different flavour profiles, tapping at various levels in the column. He might overflow the rectifier to collect more congeners for the eventual rum. He also can vary the amount of alcohol and make various types of rum in one still. These varia-

DANGER
HOT

tions are the personal approach by the master distiller and called marks. A mark usually carries a name, consisting of the initials of the master distiller followed by a number.

The rum industry uses a variety of stills. Appleton, for instance, has a three column still set-up. The first one strips the alcohol, whereas the second and third columns take care of cleaning and concentrating the distillate. Worthy Park's and Appleton's stills, by the way, were built in Scotland at Forsyth's, who reckons the majority of whisky distilleries to its clientele.

The protein-rich residue left in the stills is called "dunder". Some distilleries add dunder to the next batch, for flavour consistency; this process can be somewhat compared with the sour mash method applied by many American bourbon and Tennessee whiskey distillers. Others store the dunder in huge tanks or open ponds at the distillery. After ventilation it is used for fertilising and irrigating the sugar cane fields, resembling the recycling of pot ale in the Scottish whisky industry.

The new distillate will be sold immediately or poured in wooden barrels for maturation. Worthy Park and Appleton both prefer used barrels from white American oak. They buy large quantities from the Bluegrass Cooperage in Louisville, Kentucky. Those barrels usually previously contained Jack Daniel Tennessee whiskey. Ex-bourbon barrels from various Kentucky distillers are in use as well.

Rums mature at full strength or diluted – between 70% and 80% ABV – depending on tradition and the personal preferences of the rum blender. During maturation a chemical reaction between wood and liquid takes place, which is primarily influenced by three factors: the components, the climate and the maturation period. During fermentation and distillation esters have formed and will continue to form while the rum matures in the barrel. The first year shows an increase of colour, tannins and acids. In the following years more esters and aldehydes are formed. An ester is created by a reversible reaction between alcohol and organic acids. For example ethanol with acetic acid forms the ester ethyl acetate. Esters in a mature distillate can be recognised as fruit and flower aromas.

The master blender decides the maturation period and when to blend the rum. This blend will then rest for a while to let the rums marry well. There are hardly any single cask rums, as we know single cask whiskies. The rum bought by the consumer is virtually always a blend of different rums and/or different vintages of the same rum brand.

Rum matures three times quicker than Scottish single malt whisky, due to the subtropical climate in the Caribbean. The oldest, and very rare, single cask rum in the world is a 50-year-old Appleton expression, bottled in 2012 to celebrate the 50th anniversary of Jamaica's independence. Worldwide only 800 bottles are available, costing US $5,000 per bottle. The rum is beautifully packaged in a wooden chest. Appleton's master blender is Joy Spence, the first woman ever appointed in this craft.

The rum industry does not know central, homogenous regulations regarding labelling and packaging. Every country producing rum is, in principle, free to choose how to present its products, albeit within the framework of three different rules: Minimum Aging, Average Aging and Solera Aging. The first one is comparable with the Scottish regulations regarding the bottling and labelling of whisky. The age stated on the label always refers to the youngest rum in the blend. Appleton is one of the distillers following this rule. The second and third rules are mainly used in Latin American countries. Average means an average age of the rums blended into the end product. Solera Aging refers to blending old(er) rums with younger rums and no minimum age is required on the label. The Santa Teresa Bicentenario for example is such a blend, of which part is more than 80 years old. Strictly speaking one cannot put that age on the bottle.

The quality of the molasses, the fermentation period and the blending are the main factors that contribute to the taste and consistency of the eventual rum. Short fermentation cycles deliver light rum, longer ones produces varieties with a fuller body and taste. The master blender can blend at heart with the various marks as with the various vintages.

Producing a consistent blend time after time is very important in keeping the consumer satisfied. However, minimal differences in taste can occur. The quality of the sugar cane harvest may be influenced by the ambient temperature, the type of cane and the amount of rain fallen during growth of the crop. In a very limited manner there is a sense of "terroir".

APPLETON ESTATE DISTILLERY
PRODUCTION STATISTICS

DATE 05·07·12 CROP 2011 – 2012 CROP DAY 201

MARK	DAY ACTUAL	DAY TARGET	PREVIOUS WEEK ACTUAL	PREVIOUS WEEK TARGET	TODATE
APEL / LAA	30,009	22,500	17,963	135,000	
APCC / LAA		17,500			
APSPIS / LAA					250.1
PARAMETERS					
LAA/ TONNE	282.66	256.00	273.93	260.00	253.35
DISTILLATION POT		85.00		85.00	
EFFICIENCY COLUMN	97.70	95.00	98.04	95.00	
FERM. EFFCY.	74.4	85.00	11.49	85.00	
STEAM/LAA	17.99	8.00	12.82	8.00	

In the end three base types of rum are on the market: Dark, Amber and White. The former two are cask-matured versions, the latter isn't, unless the producing country specifies otherwise by law. When white rum does mature in casks, they are mainly older barrels, used twice or thrice before. The liquid obtains a colour, which will be filtered out with the aid of charcoal. Dark rums often receive extra colouring by the addition of small amounts of caramel.

This book is about Rum & Reggae, and implicitly about Jamaica. The rum coming from this island is traditionally made of molasses, with long fermentation cycles, natural yeast strains, distilled in a pot still. The result is a full-bodied rum with a depth of flavours.

Many more rums are made in the Caribbean. Honouring the motto "know what you drink and from where it comes" I assembled an overview of rum producing islands and countries, adding some background information. It is not complete, nor is it a tasting guide. I will leave that to the reader who, after reading this book, might get inspired to do some liquid research him or herself. In that case, Cheers! Here we go…

Antigua

A former British colony named Wadadli by the original inhabitants, meaning "our own". The island belongs to the Leewards and forms an independent unit with Barbuda and Redonda, since it separated from the British Commonwealth in 1981. English Harbour is one of its rums.

Barbados

This island belongs to the Lesser Antilles. The Spaniards discovered it in 1492 but didn't make much use of it. The same can be said of the Portuguese who arrived some 50 years later. They did release wild boars, creating a place to take in meat stock for their journeys from west to east. Only in 1624 Barbados came under British rule, continuing until November 1960. In that year it became a constitutional parliamentary democracy and part of the Commonwealth of Nations (the Commonwealth), recognising Queen Elizabeth II as head of state. A well-known Barbadian rum is Mount Gay, introduced in 1703 and the oldest rum brand in the world. Another rum from this island is Cockspur.

Belize

Situated on the northeast coast of Central America, this is not an island. It is the only country in the wide region where English is the official language, although in practice mostly Spanish is spoken. Belize is bordered by Mexico, Guatemala and the Caribbean Sea. Its original inhabitants were the Mayas, but the country was claimed by the

Spaniards during the end of the 15th century. The English and the Scots managed to establish a fort in the mid 16th century. They were called the Baymen and attacked Spanish soldiers and vessels. Around 1786 the English started to gain more power in the region and eventually in 1836 turned it into British Honduras. In 1964 independence was acquired which lead to re-baptising the country as Belize in 1973. It remains part of the Commonwealth and acknowledges Queen Elizabeth II as head of state. Since 1953 the company Travelling Liquors produces One Barrel Rum. There might have been rum made in earlier centuries. Any traces have evaporated over time.

Bermuda

Actually it's the Bermudas, since it is a cluster of islands and islets. They were named after their discoverer, the Spanish captain Juan de Bermúdez. He arrived in 1505 and found it uninhabited. By ways of the Virginia Company who set up a trading post in 1609, the area came under English influence and the population grew steadily. A small century later, in 1707, it officially became a British colony. The Bermudas, also known as the Summer Isles, are the oldest overseas country within Great Britain. Well-loved by tourists, it is also attractive as an offshore financial hub for many companies, since it has low excise tariffs. Bermuda has another claim to fame, which is the Bermuda shorts, worn by the British Army in the subtropics and the desert. They are still worn by the Royal Navy.

During the Second World War, Bermuda was confronted with a shortage of clothing. Two local entrepreneurs therefore decided to design short trousers modelling them after the British army shorts. To cover the lower part of the leg, heavy grey, knee-length woollen socks complemented the outfit. Ever since it has been the standard outfit for businessmen in the area. Later the Bermuda shorts were modernized and currently they are for sale in many fabrics and colours. The business world still maintains a strict dress code. The shorts have to be made from "suit" material and combined with a shirt, a jacket and tie.

Since 1860 Gosling has manufactured rum on Bermuda, using brand names like Black Seal, Gold Rum and Gosling's Family Reserve. In the early days the first brand was sold in champagne bottles.

British Virgin Islands

The official name is Virgin Islands. The USA and France also controlled or still control part of the islands, hence the distinction. The most important ones belonging to the British Empire are Anegada, Jost van Dyke, Tortola and Virgin Gorda. In reality it is a chain of small islands, of which part is uninhabited. They received their name from, whom else, Columbus when he discovered them in 1493, during his second voyage to the West Indies. He gave them the colourful name Saint Ursula and her 11,000 Virgins, referring to the legend of St Ursula. It didn't take long before the name was abbreviated to Las Virgines.

The Spanish conqueror didn't stay there and soon the islands became a toy of European nations who fought for control. At the time one could encounter English, Danes, French and Dutch. The latter founded a permanent establishment on Tortola in 1648 but the English kicked them out in 1672 and replaced them with sugar cane. The Virgin Islands became an important contributor to the wealth of Great Britain. Due to the abolition of slavery in the mid 19th century and a series of hurricanes, the economic climate deteriorated. The year 1967 witnessed autonomy within the British Kingdom. Today the islands are a financial and tourist's paradise. English business tycoon Richard Branson named his record label and airline after the islands, of which he actually possesses one. On Tortola Pusser's Rum is made, a reference to the purser on the English Navy vessels, who was responsible for handing out the daily tot of rum to the crew.

Cuba

Cuba cannot be neglected in a book about rum, if only for Bacardi, a story in itself. A whole tome was written about that brand alone, which originated in Cuba. The Bacardi family lost its possessions in the 1960s due to the political revolution under Fidel Castro and Che Guevara. At first the Bacardi-clan were staunch supporters of the two, but when the revolutionary tune became too communist, the Bacardi's turned away from them. As a consequence of that move the revolutionaries confiscated the Cuban possessions of the rum baron in 1960, taking those of his colleague Arechabala too.

José Pepín Bosch, at the time Bacardi's general manager, was so deeply angered that he purchased a redundant B-26 aircraft and planned to bomb the Cuban oil refineries. Rumour has it that Pepín was involved in a CIA-plot too, with the aim of murdering Castro. History shows it didn't happen. In Arechabala's old distillery today Havana Club rum is made, under the watchful eye of the government.

To avoid import taxes and due to the unstable political situation at the time, Bacardi had opened a production facility in USA controlled Puerto Rico as early as 1936. The company succeeded in converting the Bacardi brand name into a sort name, like Xerox for photocopying. The disadvantage of this was the fact that many consumers didn't recognise Bacardi as rum anymore. Cuba Libre (Bacardi with coke and lime) became a drinks category on its own. In recent years Bacardi has done its utmost to revert that image and emphasises in ad campaigns that it is rum originating from Cuba. A few times the company received reprimands from various institutions regarding misleading advertisements.

Bacardi's logo is a bat. According to legend this animal lived in the attic of the Cuban building where Facundo Bacardi started making rum on a commercial scale in 1862. He had done some experimenting first with cask maturation and charcoal filtering. His aim was to make a smooth, light rum. He allegedly presented the first white rum to the world market.

Outside Cuba the Bacardi company started to produce its own Havana Club, for the US market. After all, the latter country does not import Cuban products. Since Castro and company had taken Havana Club distillery after the Cuban Revolution, the original brand owner, Mr Arecha-bala, never registered the brand name in the USA. Knowing this, Bacardi saw no harm in releasing a second version of Havana Club rum. Apparently the feelings of revenge had not dwindled away after the ill-fated B-26 adventure. The brand introduction obviously led to confusion for the consumer. To make things even more complicated: the for-mer Bacardi distillery in Cuba still makes rum, known as Caney. Of course Bacardi's own rums are not imported and sold in Cuba, not a single drop. Years later Fidel Castro would remark: "At the time we never thought about reg-istering the Bacardi brand and so we lost it. We did own the plant where the original Bacardi rum was made, but we were not allowed to use the name."

The Cuban government cooperates with the French company Pernod-Ricard to sell their version of Havana Club outside the USA and the American territories. So, when in The Netherlands I savour the Cuban version and in our American dwelling the Bacardi version. Not only its political approach, but also its taste differs.

Bacardi is still family owned and led by Facundo's great-grandson. Its headquarters stand proudly in Miami, Florida.

Dominican Republic
The island of Hispaniola is subdivided into two different countries – 1/3 in the west, called Haiti and 2/3 in the east, named Dominican Republic. Columbus, him again,

showed up in 1492 and took it for Spain, which country continued to occupy Hispaniola for three centuries. The Haitian part came under the influence of the French. The island witnessed the first huge slave revolts and that might have been one of the causes why the Dominican Republic turned independent as early as 1821. The capital Santo Domingo is host to the first cathedral in the region, as well as the first castle. That's why it ended up on the UN-ESCO World Heritage List. Through internal quarrels with their neighbours the country relinquished to Spain again in 1844. Then the USA became the new occupants until 1924. A few years of relative rest followed, after which a dictator seized power, a revolt culminating in a civil war in 1961. One dictator was swapped for another but since 1978 it is democratically led, more or less. The political situation remains unstable. Where sugar cane used to be the main source of income on the island, today it is business services and tourism. The island still produces rums, of which Brugal is the best known, flanked by Barceló and Bermúdez.

Guyana

This is not an island, but together with Belize the only part of the continent in Central and South America that is reckoned to belong to the Caribbean. Way back when it was a Dutch colony, then taken by the English, who called it British Guyana for a long time. In 1966 independence was celebrated and on the 23rd of February 1971, Guyana declared itself a republic, but remained part of the Commonwealth. Self-acclaimed high priest Jim Jones shocked the world in 1978, when, under his spiritual guidance, more than 900 members of his Peoples Temple sect committed collective suicide in Jonestown.

Guyana is famous for its Demerara rums, made of Demerara sugar, named after the province and the river that flows through the country for 226 miles, before reaching the Atlantic Ocean. When the Dutch invaded Guyana around 1611, Demerara was a country of its own. Nature here overflows with an abundance of flora and fauna species, partly because the country has one of the largest unspoilt rain forests in the world.

No wonder Sir Walter Raleigh, and in his footsteps Sir David Attenborough, felt so attracted to it. Some years ago the BBC dedicated a beautiful documentary in three parts to Guyana, titled *Lost Land of the Jaguar.*

At one time more than 200 distilleries dotted the countryside. Shortly after the declaration of independence, in 1971, only three were left. Now it is reduced to one – Diamond. If you want to do a vertical tasting of rums, try El Dorado with bottled vintages of 5, 12, 15, 21 and 25 years old.

Haiti

In the 17th century the western part of Hispaniola was frequented by French pirates, led by Bertrand d'Ogeran. He decided to stay and grow tobacco, becoming a role model for other buccaneers. They were at war with the Spanish in the eastern part and many a clash occurred. In 1697

France and Spain settled their quarrels and divided the island officially in two. At first the French named their part Saint Domingue, not to be confused with Santo Domingo, the current capital of the Dominican Republic. The following century saw many French colonists settling on the island, trying to make their fortune with exploiting sugar cane plantations. Slaves were imported on a seriously grand scale, which resulted around 1790 in a ratio of 1:10 free versus slave.

This situation was bound to turn unstable and a year later, inspired by the French Revolution from 1789, a huge slave revolt took place. Numerous French expats were butchered and whole families fled to the USA, among others to Charleston, SC and New Orleans, LA, both with French Quarters dating to earlier French merchant settlements.

The British planned an invasion in 1793 but had to succumb to the former slaves, whose leader Toussaint Louverture managed to make peace between the warring factions in 1794. He not only chased away the Spaniards and the French, but the English too, after which stunt he undisturbedly opened trade negotiations with the defeated nations as well as with the USA.

In 1802 it was the turn of the French to try and get the island back, but they had to give up at the end of 1803 and withdrew their last troops, about 7,000 in total, from the island. One could say this was Napoleon's Caribbean Waterloo.

Rum

On January 1, 1814 the independent republic "Ay-iti" was established, the Arawak expression for "mother earth". With that historical deed Haiti became the only nation in the world that grew out of a slave revolt. 1825 witnessed a second attempt by the French to re-posses their lost "property", but this time President Boyer decided to buy them off. After having received 150 million francs, the French promised to acknowledge Haiti's independence. The amount paid was cruelly earmarked as "compensation for the loss of the slave trade". The French abolitionist Victor Schoelcher put it this way: the inhabitants had to pay with money for what they already had paid for with their blood.

As a consequence Haiti was covered in huge debts, eventually leading to an American occupation, from 1915-1934. Then Haiti became a dictatorship, with its dreaded and hated exponents Papa Doc and Baby Doc. The latter was succeeded by Aristide, who himself was thrown out of power by a coup. The population grew poorer and poorer. The years 2010 and 2011 hit the inhabitants harshly with various natural disasters and diseases.

It sometimes seems the poorest country in the world is doomed. Miraculously rum is still made here. Barbancourt was founded on March 18, 1862 and has not stopped producing an eponymous rum, among which a rare 15-year-old expression. The founder and originator of the name originally came from Charente, the French region where cognac is made...

Guadeloupe

This is a Caribbean island that belongs to the European Union, true! It's still French and one can pay with euros. Of course it was the unavoidable Columbus who first discovered the island, in 1493, and the story goes he there became acquainted with the pineapple, a crop that had been growing in South America for centuries. In 1674 the French managed to steal Guadeloupe from the Spanish, but had to succumb to the English during the further course of the 17th century. In 1763 it returned into French hands as part of the Treaty of Paris, in exchange for parts of Canada. On this island rum is made from sugar cane juice, as the French are accustomed to do. They call it rhum agricole or rhum traditionelle. Known brands are Damoiseau, Karukera and Montebello.

Jamaica

With a whole chapter about this island, I limit myself here to mentioning their best-known rums. Apart from Appleton, there is Wray & Nephew (W&N), Rum Bar Rum, Worthy Gold, Myers and a series of private label rums, among which Coruba, especially made for New Zealand. Diageo partly owns a distillery at Clarendon in southern Jamaica via a joint venture with National Rums of Jamaica for making Captain Morgan. W&N and Rum Bar Rum are overproof white rums, typical for Jamaica – Rough and Tough. Something to which we can testify, since we were initiated into Jamaican rum-drinking habits with it upon arrival at our hotel in Greenwood, east of Montego Bay – strong stuff!

Martinique

The French speaking Martinique's also use the juice instead of molasses and ferment it in a controlled environment. Various types of stills are used for distilling. End products are called rhum agricole – as the French somewhat arrogantly call their product, as if other rums would not be agricultural – and industrial alcohol. Well-known brands are Clement and Depaz. A short while ago Martinique received its own appellation, to describe a specific terroir, as is common practise with (French) wines.

Puerto Rico

Again, Columbus cannot be avoided. During his second voyage to the West Indies he must have anchored in many bays, since the archipelago of Puerto Rico also shows up on his list of honour. As their favourite modus operandi, the Spanish took control of the island and murdered the indigenous population, unwittingly using early forms of biological warfare by introducing European infectious diseases against which the islanders had no natural resistance.

Despite many attacks by the French, English and Dutch, the Spanish persisted in control for over four centuries. Only in 1898 Spain lost the islands to the USA, in the Spanish-American War. Since 1917 Puerto Ricans have been officially recognised as American citizens, albeit that they cannot vote to elect the president, since they are not one of the 50 states, but rather "an unincorporated territory of the United States." It's a status currently being dis-

J. WRAY

SUGAR FAC

NEPHEW LTD

& DISTILLERY

cussed, after the referendum held on November 6, 2012. Over 61% of the population voted for statehood. It remains to be seen if that is going to happen.

Bacardi rum is made in Puerto Rico, as is Ron del Barrilito, Don Q and Captain Morgan. The latter brand was introduced by then-owner Seagram in 1944 and originally produced in Jamaica. Due to the attractive tax structure, Seagram built a huge distillery in Puerto Rico during the 1950s, following Bacardi's example. At the same time Seagram acquired the rights to distribute Captain Morgan in Puerto Rico and subsequently mentioned on the label "product of Puerto Rico". However the pirate Henry Morgan was closely connected to Jamaica, both culturally and historically. In 2001 the Captain's brand was acquired by Diageo, which company also owns a distillery in St Croix, one of the US Virgin Islands.

St Kitts and Nevis
Two little islands that form an independent state since 1983 within the Commonwealth, with Queen Elizabeth II as head of state. St Kitts is the first mooring place of the English and French colonists and therefore also known as the Mother Colony of the West Indies. The name is derived from San Cristobal, given to it by the omnipresent Columbus, in 1498. He called the other island Nuestra Senora de las Nieves, in plain English Our Lady of the Snow, referring to a 4th century miracle, when snow fell in Rome, Italy. Anyway, the famous Ben Nevis in Scotland has nothing to do with it, notwithstanding that its peak is often covered

in snow. The island Nevis is naturally not acquainted with the icy white dusting, but its highest elevation, Nevis Peak, is regularly hidden in the clouds.

Many remnants of sugar plantations can be spotted on St Kitts, but the sugar cane fields had to make way for building houses. Currently tourism is the main stream of income for the island. The only remaining sugar factory was closed in 2005. One distillery is still active, producing alcohol that was sold as Cane Spirit Rothschild (CSR). Nowadays it is a joint venture with Demerara Distillers from Guyana, for which company Belmont Estate Rum is blended and bottled. Another rum brand is Brinley.

St Lucia
The French named this island after Saint Lucy of Syracuse, after they colonised it in 1660. She is the patron saint of the blind and her name is derived from the Latin "lux", meaning light. It comes as no surprise that the island carries the motto "The Land, The People, The Light". No less than 14 times the French and the English fought over possession and it changed hands that many times. In 1814 it definitely became part of the British Empire, to gain a state of independence within the Commonwealth from 1979. St Lucia Distillers produces a whole series of rums, among which Chairman's Reserve, Admiral Rodney and Bounty.

Trinidad & Tobago
These two islands are part of an archipelago with numerous islets. Trinidad is by far the most prosperous. Becom-

ing a Spanish colony in 1498, it was taken by the British on February 18, 1797, with a huge fleet of war ships. Tobago continued to be a toy over which the Spaniards, French, English and Dutch quarrelled but eventually it was incorporated in the British Empire in 1802. In the early 1960s the islands became independent and 1976 saw the declaration of the republic. Rare for a Caribbean island is its extensive petrochemical industry. The islands allegedly are the birthplace of the limbo dance and calypso, one of the musical influences heard in Jamaican mento, a predecessor of reggae. Trinidad & Tobago is where the famous Angostura bitters and eponymous rum are made.

Angostura is owned by CL Financial, a conglomerate that also owns the Scottish single malt whisky distilleries Deanston, Bunnahabhain and Tobermory. Another rum made on the islands is 10 Cane, owned by Moët Hennessy.

US Virgin Islands
Once Danish property, this group of islands was sold by Denmark to the USA for the princely sum of 25 million dollars. The largest of the islands is called St Croix, the most easterly part of the USA. Its history is marinated in migrations, resulting a form of Spanglish – Puerto Rican Spanish mixed with the local Crucian dialect. The original inhabitants were known as Cruzan. Hence the Cruzan Distillery, founded in 1760, still going strong, where, apart from rum, Southern Comfort is made.

Recently Diageo put a distillery on the island and produces rum for its flagship Captain Morgan, which, understandably, is not well appreciated in Puerto Rico.

William Grant & Sons, owner of Glenfiddich and Balvenie single malts, is present with Sailor Jerry rum, named after the legendary tattoo artist and sailor Norman Collins. He joined the American Navy in 1930 and during his many trips to Southeast Asia and the Pacific he became lifelong infatuated with the art of tattooing. After his departure in 1961 his protégés Ed Hardy and Mike Malone continued where he left off. Malone died in 2007. Hardy became a phenomenon in the tattoo world and is famous for his body art. Sailor Jerry lives on as a bottle of rum, made by a Scottish enterprise in the Caribbean. The label was designed after a tattoo depicting a female inhabitant of the Pacific.

***

Outside the Caribbean, rum is made as well. The most important producers can be found in Central and South America.

Argentina

Once upon a time discovered by the Spaniards, Argentina received its name from them because they hoped to mine silver in the country (the Latin word for silver is argentum). However, to their dismay, silver was nowhere to be found. For centuries Argentina would be the stage for many battles between foreign powers, suffered under the yoke of military juntas, but nowadays seems to be in quieter political waters. It celebrates three world famous icons: newly elected Pope Francis I, star football player Lionel Messi and Princess Maxima, married to Crown Prince William Alexander of the Kingdom of the Netherlands. And rum, made in the town of Tucumán. Isla N Rum is produced in pot stills and matured in French oak casks.

Brazil

Forget about Columbus for a change. The Portuguese were the first Europeans to land here. From 1500 until 1815, Brazil was a colony after which it became part of the Kingdom of Portugal, for only seven years. 1822 brought independence, which took the Portuguese three years to recognise. Currently it is a republic.

The names stems from "brazil wood", a tree shedding a strong red colour used as paint in the clothing industry and considered the first export product to Europe in the 16th century. The Portuguese knew about sugar cane and how to grow it, having importing it to Madeira and the Azores, from where it might have been taken to Brazil.

Here, as on the French-Caribbean islands, the distillate is made of sugar cane juice instead of molasses. It goes by the name of cachaça and for a long time was billed as Brazilian rum, the correctness often disputed, since extra sugar and even corn meal is sometimes added.

On April 9, 2012, the discussion ended when cachaça was officially recognised as an indigenous Brazilian drink. In other words, the distillate received an appellation. Locals consume cachaça with raw sugar and lime. This drink is called Caipirinha. Famous brands are Leblon, Pitú, Sagat-iba and Ypioca. However Brazil also produces traditional rum from molasses, of which Oronoco is an example.

Ecuador
Around 1463, the Republic of the Equator was incorporat-ed into the Empire of the Incas, led by Huayna Capac, after having been a battlefield between various peoples for cen-turies. When Capac died in 1525 the empire was divided into a northern and a southern half between his sons Ata-hualpa and Huáscar. The former wasn't particularly happy about that and decided to kill his brother in 1530, after which event he reunited both halves of the country.

He didn't enjoy his empire for long. The Spanish con-quistadores arrested and executed him for murdering his brother – seems rather like the pot calling the kettle black. After 300 years of uninterrupted Spanish occupation, Ec-uador gained independence in 1822 and became part of Simón Bolívar's short-lived Republic of Gran Colombia, embracing Venezuela and Colombia too. Ecuador left that combination in 1830 to become a sole republic, which it still is. Estelar is a well-known rum made here.

Guatemala
This is the land of the much-coveted Ron Zacapa. Ron is the Spanish way to write rum. Zacapa is made out of the first pressing of the sugar cane – virgin sugar cane honey, as olive oil from the first pressing is called virgin. A solera system is used for maturation, comparable with the sys-

tem applied by the sherry bodegas of Spain.

The numbers on the labels seem to mention the age of the rum, but that is deceptive. Zacapa 23 for instance is a blend of rums aged between six and 23 years. Zacapa 15 is a blend with rums between five and 15 years of age. Apparently they find no harm in emphasising the oldest rum and the law of the land does not prohibit this practise. Regardless of its real age, Zacapa is held in high esteem internationally.

The country itself, home to the Mayan culture, was colonised by the Spanish but joined the Mexican empire in 1821. The latter dissolved a mere two years later. Then dictators came and went. Some rose to power with outside help, notably from American companies. Such was the case with the United Fruit Company (UFC) from New Orleans, Louisiana. This enterprise controlled vast properties in Central and South America, during the first half of the 20th century – mainly banana plantations.

The UFC is the forerunner of current Chiquita Brands International, which was built on the back of Guatemala. The second half of the 20th century witnessed a long civil war, a series of coupes and guerrilla attacks.

The feuds ended in 1996, with the help of Spain and Norway (!). Today Guatemala is a presidential constitutional republic. Remarkably some excellent rums arise from this former banana republic. Zacapa is produced at Licoreras de Guatemala, also home to another series of rums, known as Ron Botran.

Nicaragua

The land that can boast the finding place of 2,000 year old human foot prints has always been a hotbed of struggles, terrorist and guerrilla activities, which led to more than one international intervention in the past. Former US president Ronald Reagan (1981-1989) once ventilated his concern regarding the growing Russian and Cuban influence in Nicaragua, pointing at the danger of "a second Cuba".

Nicaragua also is the country of the Contras and the Sandinistas who ended the Somoza era, led by their Hauptman Daniel Ortega. But probably what made the country most (in)famous was the USA weapon scandal during the Reagan administration. In a secret, covert operation weapons were sold to Iran to help release American hostages in Lebanon. The proceeds were then diverted to support the Contras, something that had been forbidden by Congress.

Eventually things were found out and Lieutenant-Colonel Oliver North would become the national scapegoat for this scandalous case of "international intervention".

In 1990 the Sandinista junta was overthrown by Violetta Chamorro, who soon saw the country sliding into the abyss. Earlier the USA had threatened with an enduring trade boycott, partly having caused the local economy to deteriorate, should the Sandinistas again govern. Daniel Ortega did try several times to regain power, regardless of the fact that the US government kept warning him and his Sandinistas. Despite that formidable opposition, Ortega managed to be elected president of the republic again. He was inaugurated on January 10, 2012.

All that hassle did not intervene with the making of rum, reckoned to belong to the best in Latin America. Flor de Cana has been producing a series of rums since 1937, varying in age between four and 18 years.

Panama

First discovered in the 16th century by the Spaniards, Panama threw off the yoke in 1821. At first the country participated in the union of Gran Colombia, then from 1831 it became a more or less independent province of Nueva Granada (which would later become Colombia) and eventually it reached total independence in 1903, with the help of the USA. The latter assisted with its US Army Corps of Engineers in building the Panama Canal between 1904 and 1917. Coincidentally large numbers of Jamaicans were hired, too. Controlling the canal was important to all concerned, since the toll paid by passing ships was a major stream of income.

One source mentions Panama meaning "many butterflies"; another insists on "many fish". Panama started as a constitutional democracy, but military juntas ended that situation. Eventually the USA interfered with Operation Just Cause, to secure its interests in the Panama Canal and to depose the junta, led by Manuel Noriega. He supposedly earned his money with drug trafficking and "importing" Chinese labourers. Noriega was caught and sentenced. Today Panama is a republic.

Since 1908 Varele Hermanos SA produces rum from sugar cane juice, with brand names such as Ron Abuelo,

Ron Cortez and Seco Herrerano. Other brands made in the country are Malecon and Ron de Jeremy.

Surinam(e)

From 1667 until 1975 Surinam was a Dutch colony and named Dutch Guiana. The name Surinam was originally given by the English colonists, before the Dutch swapped the country with them in exchange for a tiny trade post in North America, at the time listening to the name New Amsterdam – the predecessor of latter day New York.

The Dutch added an "e" to their new colony's name and exploited coffee, cacao, sugar and cotton plantations, with the help of forced labour: in other words, African slaves. They were treated badly and many ran off into the rain forests where they managed to create their own culture.

Between 1863 and 1873 slavery was abolished, step-by-step. To compensate for the loss of its "employees" the Netherlands contracted workers from the Dutch East Indies and India. That's why the relatively small population has such a rich ethnic background.

During the Second World War the Dutch government requested the USA to temporarily occupy Suriname, in order to protect the bauxite mines. In 1973 negotiations were begun, that ended two years later in independence for Suriname. Every citizen was offered a choice either to stay or to emigrate to the Netherlands. Many left for Amsterdam, which still has a large population of Surinam Dutch citizens.

The Netherlands and rum mainly built up a relation in trading and blending, not so much in manufacturing the drink. Suriname however does make its own rum. The most well-known brand is Borgoe, produced since 1982, just seven years after the country became independent. Suriname Alcoholic Beverages NV also makes Black Cat and Marienburg rum.

Venezuela

After fierce battles with the indigenous population, Spain succeeded in colonising the country in 1522. It took 290 years to become the first Spanish-American colony announcing independence, which was effected a mere 10 years later, in 1821, by participating in the Republic of Colombia. In 1830 total independence was established. Dictators came and went in a rapid pace, until the mid 20th century, a relatively democratic period in its existence. The quiet times ended in the 1980s caused by a deteriorating economy and the deposing of president Perez, who illegally subsidised his income by robbing the nation's treasure chest. 1998 saw the rise of former military officer Hugo Chávez, who gave Venezuela a new constitution.

The Republic of Venezuela consists of 23 states. Because of its natural oil reserves it is one of the wealthiest countries in the region. It possesses huge stocks and exports at length. Chávez is a controversial president but was re-elected in 2012.

The country itself had been discovered in 1499 by Alonso de Ojeda who had offered Florentine citizen Amerigo Vespucci a lift to Guyana. The name giver of North and South America called Alonso's discovery "little Venice". The houses on wooden poles, amidst flowing water, reminded him of the eponymous city in Italy.

Cacique was founded in 1953 and is the best selling rum in Venezuela. Pampero is slightly older (1938) and a local favourite, with large exports to Europe, mainly Italy and Spain. The Venezuelans call the latter brand Caballito Frenao, the rearing horse, which is the logo on the bottle. That nickname is their synonym for rum.

***

The Caribbean, Central and South America are important players on the world market for rum. However, there are many more places on the globe where rum is produced, or at least a drink carrying that name, not always with sugar cane at its heart.

In the back of this book you can find an extensive list of brands, organised alphabetically as well as geographically. It is not a complete overview, since new brands are introduced annually and some might have been taken off the market after publication of this work.

Countries that cannot grow sugar cane might make rum and import either molasses or bulk rum, distilled and blended by specialist companies. One of the largest rum blenders in the world is the aforementioned company E&A Scheer, based in Amsterdam. They have been around for over 300 years and also produce arrack, which is called

East-Indian rum by some, rice brandy by others. It is a logical thing, knowing the Dutch were present in the East Indies for centuries and once held Indonesia as a mighty colony, until it declared itself independent in 1945. That act turned into an armed conflict – The Indonesian National Revolution. After four years of fierce battle the Dutch finally acknowledged Indonesia's independence at the end of 1949.

***

When I savour a glass of rum, I prefer not to listen to my musical loves Blues & Jazz, but instead to the music that is unmistakably tied to Jamaica, and with rum: Reggae.

How was that musical style created and from where did superstar and world famous reggae icon Bob Marley actually come? Well, pour yourself a nice glass and dissolve in riddim. No fear, mon!

Rum Types

Light rum

Also: silver or white rum. Very suitable for use in cocktails, because of its sweetish unobtrusive taste.

Gold rum

Also: amber. Heavier bodied. The colour comes from cask maturation and the taste is fuller than that of white rum.

Dark rum

Also: red, brown, black. A full-bodied blend of mature rums, abundant with flavours. Excellent for use in the kitchen, too. Haiti, Jamaica and Martinique are known for producing dark rums, as are Guatemala and Nicaragua.

Spiced rum

Base: golden and light rums. Addition of spices like aniseed, cinnamon, pepper and rosemary. Caramel colouring might be added, especially with the light rums.

Flavoured rum

Rum infused with banana, coconut, lime, orange or mango. Usually less than 40% ABV. Fine for mixing drinks; can also be enjoyed pure or over ice.

Overproof rum

White rums ranging from 57.5% to 80% ABV. A famous one is Wray & Nephew Overproof, loved by Jamaicans. Our initiation drink when we arrived on the island.

Premium rum

Very rich in aromas and flavours; usually a blend of old(er) rums. Ultimatum Infinitum 25, made by Dutch drinks specialist Jan Beek, is a fine example.

REGGAE

Reggae

Reggae – *a style of popular music with a strongly accented subsidiary beat, originating in Jamaica. Reggae evolved in the late 1960s from ska and other local variations on calypso and rhythm & blues, and became widely known in the 1970s through the work of Bob Marley; its lyrics are much influenced by Rastafarian ideas.*

Afterbeat – *accentuating the second and fourth count in quadruple time (four/four), especially by the accompanying instruments. Contrary to the standard accents in western music emphasised on the first and third count. The use of the afterbeat is typical for reggae music.*

The word reggae was first used, albeit in a somewhat different spelling, by Toots Hibbert of Toots & The Maytals, in their 1968 song "Do the Reggay". The man himself once said about that: "I didn't invent it, it just happened, and then I wrote the song from pure inspiration. Before that time we called our music ska, or bluebeat, or rocksteady. I didn't know what I was doing, really, but reggae was a word we were using, and so it just happens that I was the one who put the R in the music."

Reggae undisputedly is the essence of Jamaican music, although the island does have a long musical tradition. The Arawak hacked and gouged their drums out of tree trunks and spanned them with the elastic skin of the manatee.

They also cut primitive flutes from twigs, small branches and animal bones. Those rudimentary instruments were primarily used during religious rituals and funerals.

The West Africans who where transported to the Caribbean as slaves brought their own musical styles some 800 years and played the burru – a set of three drums. The atumpan acts as the soprano drum with a free role and is accompanied by the apentemma and the petia, respectively the alto and bass drums. They were used in combination with rattles and bottles. At the time, when a slave survived prison or a severe whipping, he would be loudly welcomed with a concert.

The influx of migrants from Scotland and Ireland, mainly in the 19th century, added another dimension to the indigenous music, since the banished Celts brought their reels, bodhrans, pipes and fifes with them.

Jamaicans, who had worked on the Panama Canal in the early 20th century, came in touch with musical styles such as the tango, samba and calypso. They would take these music forms home. Styles and influences were put together and blended into the typical Jamaican mento style – a syncopated rhythm somewhat like the rumba, on a European chord structure. In *Bourbon & Blues* I described the difference between the African pentatonic and European diatonic chord sequences, so I won't elaborate on that subject here.

Mento would be the major Jamaican musical style until ska emerged in the mid 1950s. To better understand the development from mento to reggae it is worthwhile and unavoidable to make a pit stop at American Rhythm & Blues and the DJ culture.

Jamaicans love a strong beat and a pounding bass. Friends and family who temporarily left the island during World War II, when the economy was not too strong, lived in South America and the American South, and upon their return took Latin jazz and American R&B records back to Jamaica.

The musicians at home immediately picked up these styles and blended them into mento, evolving into ska some time later. The roots of the latter word are fodder for discussion. Various Jamaican musicians claim its introduction in the musical language. Among them are guitarist Ernest Ranglin and bass players Cluett Johnson and Byron Lee. Singer Derrick Morgan, from Jamaica too, explained its existence as follows: "The guitar and piano make a sound like ska, ska. That's why we call the music ska."

In the 1950s it was far from easy to play for live radio, let alone to have your song recorded. Instead people played purchased records on so-called Sound Systems, a primitive portable discotheque. Put a couple of speakers, amplifiers and a turntable on an old pickup truck and you are assured of a good time in the open air, with great music and dancing.

Soon the owners of the Sound Systems started to compete seriously, influenced by new technology with stronger amplifiers and more powerful speakers. The men who ran them chose fancy names like Tom The Great Sebastian, Duke Reid, Sir Coxsone and King Edwards, to name a

few. These were colourful characters. Especially The Duke would come to the fore, an ex-cop who, according to many, had strong ties with the criminal side of society, dressed flamboyantly and always carrying a loaded gun. His body-guards literally carried him when Reid performed as a DJ. They put him on their shoulders and walked him to the turntable where he would smoothly play one record after another, changing the vinyl with his gold-ringed fingers.

Duke's big competitor was Sir Coxsone, birth name Clement Dodd, his nickname a reference to a famous con-temporary cricket player. Dodd earned it, since he was a good player himself.

Both adversaries were known to hire bodyguards and send them to the other's "concert" in order to intimidate visitors. On some occasions real life-and-death battles were fought, with knifes drawn and pistols fired. Spies from both sides would try to find out which records were played by either Reid or Coxsone. The one with the best tune owned the crowd for the evening. To hide what re-cord was on the turntable, the name of the song and the performing artist were meticulously crossed out, after which a new fancy name was put in place. "Coxsone's Hop" for instance was actually "Later for Gator" by the Ameri-can saxophone player Willis Gatortail Jackson.

This was plain piracy and counterfeiting. It must be said however that the song would render a lot of attention since it was played so often. On the other hand, when song and performer's name have been altered, you won't profit a single dime as the original author. The Sound System owners considered it common practise after a while and the competition grew fiercer.

At first, both men would play the records themselves, but soon they hired DJs, who would become famous in their own right. One of them, Prince Buster, starting out as a body guard for Tom the Great Sebastian, set up his own shop later and gained a place between titans Reid and Coxsone. Buster was a fairly good boxer, which added to his status. Years later his fame would grow considerably when he founded a record company and a radio station called Voice of the People.

The most important DJ of the early days of the Sound Systems was Count Matchuki. He is considered the godfather of "toasting". Like Prince Buster, the Count started with Tom the Great Sebastian, but transferred to Sir Coxsone within a few years. Not an unusual move, since the bosses always tried to lure successful DJs away from their competitors. In this particular case Sebastian had been so intimidated by the Duke and his henchmen that he opted for a back seat. Count Matchuki (also spelled Machuki) needed a challenge and after a short stint with Tokyo the Monarch (another one of those beautifully chosen nicknames) ended up with Coxsone.

The Count then introduced "talking over the sound of the record", referred to as toasting. According to himself he picked up the idea from the magazine *Jive*. Not long after that moment he wrote his first "jive":

If you dig my jive
You're cool and very much alive
Everybody all around town
Machuki is the reason why I shake it down
When it comes to jive
You can't whip him with no stick

Besides toasting he made unique sounds in the micro-
phone. At first the audience believed those sound bites to
be part of the original recording but soon they understood
the Count was responsible for adding them. It immediately
caught on.

Picture the mid 1950s when the Count introduced
these novelties. Without exaggeration it can be said that he
laid the basis for rap. In Jamaica Matchuki is often called
"The Original DJ". Winston Cooper, his birth name, had a
habit of chewing on a matchstick and that stuck to him as
it were. He died in 1995 and has been hugely influential for
later reggae, rap and dub musicians, among whom U-Roy
and Snoop Dogg. During Matchuki's heyday more famous
DJs played the circuit, such as King Sporty and King Stitt.
The latter was born deformed and turned that fact into a
marketing tool, dubbing himself "The Ugly One".

The record selectors and sound engineers also played
an important role in the development of the Sound Systems. They made the sound, not only by choosing the right
records but also with assembling and fine-tuning the music installation. Lee "Scratch" Perry and King Tubby cannot
be overlooked, even more because they would grow into

skilful producers, leaving their own, significant mark on reggae, about which more in a moment.

Although the Sound Systems, competitive as they were, filled a huge longing for the Jamaican population, the performing part wanted to hear a recording of their own. The portable pick up – turntable, amplifier and speaker in one (usually the lid) became affordable. Duke and Coxsone had to discover an answer to that development. They found one in starting their own recording studios, although at first they weren't too enthusiastic about such ventures. After a hesitant beginning, Coxsone's Studio One would become a real cradle of talent and spawned the original three Wailers – Bob Marley, Peter Tosh and Bunny Livingstone – who recorded plenty of their early work in that place.

Slowly mento began to change. The rhythm was accentuated and brass instruments were added. In R&B it is quite common to emphasise the unaccented 2nd and 4th count in a four/four. Jamaican musicians – influenced by the songs of Professor Longhair and Fats Domino, whose records were played continuously on the Sound Systems – took this habit a step further and used the horn section to only play the accents. When well performed, it was known as "skanking", comparable with swing in jazz. Later guitar and keyboard took over that function, since this technique is especially fatiguing for horn players. The drummer used the bass drum on the 2nd and 4th count, combined with the snare drum. This sounds as if the 1st count falls away. That's why this is called "one drop" in the music world.

Now, after the emergence of mento, another musical growing period on the way to reggae was added: ska! Dancing to these new, fast and lively tunes was also called skanking. During my research for this book I found a delightful description of the dance, unfortunately without the original source mentioned, but it is too good to leave out, so here it comes: "Walking without moving forward, combined with milking an imaginary cow." In the 1980s, when the ska fury in Jamaica had passed, the British band Madness kindled a short-lived ska revival with songs like "One Step Beyond". The name of the band as well as the song are a direct reference to Prince Buster, the old time sound engineer and DJ. And indeed, when looking at the YouTube clip of Madness, it is not difficult to see that cow while not gaining an inch of ground. Check out: http://www.youtube.com/watch?v=N-uyWAe0NhQ. However, the 80s revival-ska was much sharper and pointier than the original Jamaican ska.

Let's return to Kingston in 1962. On 6 August Jamaica finally gained its full independence. That important step for the country also boosted the musical conscience of the Jamaicans, witnessed by the release of Jimmy Cliff's single "Miss Jamaica". In Coxsone's Studio One a respected group of local musicians united themselves in the Skatalites, quickly becoming the hottest ska ticket on the island. Among them were composer and organ player Jackie Mitto, and a fantastic trombone player, Don Drummond. Unfortunately he killed his girlfriend in 1965, claiming temporary insanity and was locked up in a psychiatric ward. Four years later he would die under mysterious circumstances. Some said of malnutrition, some said of revenge.

Master guitar player Ernest Ranglin often joined the ranks and they recorded a huge UK-hit – "Guns of Navarone". The Skatalites also performed as studio musicians for other acts. They can be heard on the first Jamaican Wailers hit, the ska song "Simmer Down" from 1963. The text is a straight reference to the behaviour of the "rude boys", violent youngsters in Jamaica's townships, borne out of the small groups of bodyguards who had been intimidating visitors to the Sound Systems in the early days. A very young Bob Marley, not a Rastafarian yet, already preached tolerance.

Sadly the rude boys became tools in the fierce election battles between the PNP and the JLP. Many years later some of them would try to assassinate both Bob Marley and Peter Tosh. Gangsta rap, a later musical form of expression, is directly derived from the behaviour and the clothing style of those angry young men.

Not only Sir Coxsone and Duke Reid ventured into recording music. More Jamaicans set up studios and record companies, the likes of Leslie Kong, Ken Khouri, Edward Seaga (who would later become a JLP Prime Minister for Jamaica) and Chris Blackwell. The latter, a white Jamaican, is the founder of Island Records, which headquarters he moved to London in 1962. From there he not only produced records of his own artists, but also arranged distribution of music recorded by his competitors in Jamaica. Blackwell was on his way to becoming a very important figure in the world of reggae and other popular music.

The ska rage in Jamaica simmered down in 1966, when the dancing crowds at the Sound System concerts grew tired of the up tempo songs and longed after a slower variation on the tune. They found the answer in rocksteady, slower than ska with a prominent role for the bass guitar. Where ska is recognisable in its walking bass, the instrument takes a counterpoint position in rocksteady, opposing the rhythm of guitar and keyboards. At roughly the same time soul music began to trickle down from the USA and added its own flavour. Three- member-choirs replaced the horn section and many tunes were actually love songs.

It can be disputed who recorded the first rocksteady song. Some candidates are "Girl I've Got a Date" by Alton Ellis and "Take it Easy" by Hopeton Lewis. Aretha Franklin's awesome song "Rock Steady" might have been a fine winner, if not for the fact that she launched the song in 1971 when rocksteady in Jamaica was largely a station passed. The clear soul and funk influences were immediately and cordially embraced by the Jamaicans.

The great guitarist and bandleader Lyn Taitt claims the invention of rocksteady as a musical genre. According to his then piano player Gladstone Anderson, in 1964 he switched into lower gear when recording "Take it Easy". Decades later Taitt would confirm this in an interview held in 2002, while adding: "actually rocksteady is a slow form of ska". The rocksteady period only lasted a couple of years. Famous bands from that era were The Paragons, The Silvertones and The Techniques.

With the influx of young people who exchanged the

countryside for Kingston, ending up in the poor ghettos of Rivertown, Trenchtown and Greenwich Town, social unrest started to fester. The unemployment rate was huge and crime seemed an attractive alternative way of living to many. With their cool style of living, they sank down into the underclass of rude boys who fought one another in hand-to-hand combat, often ending in dead victims. They became, as already mentioned, willing tools for the government in the JLP-PNP battle. Rocksteady songs at the end of the boom contain many references to the rude boys, like "Rude Boy Gone a Jail" and "Don't be a Rude Boy".

Still, the short-lived rocksteady style has been very important for the existence of reggae. Its prominent bass line was pioneered in rocksteady and many reggae musicians who grew to fame in the 1970s used to play in ska and rocksteady bands. The evolution in recording techniques, which offered the studios multi-track recording, led to experimenting with different arrangements, in which various instruments would alternatively take the lead. Bass playing became more complex and the piano was exchanged for the electric organ. Horn players were directed to the back of the sage while the rhythm guitar began to emphasise the offbeat.

At the same time, fuelled by the social unrest in the Caribbean and the USA, the Rastafarian movement gained ground. Where old timers like Coxsone and Reid thoroughly disliked its followers – on the one hand for their "dreadful" looks, on the other hand for their affinity with smoking ganja – more progressive producers opened the doors for the Rasta musicians.

A few years later Coxsone turned and opened the doors of Studio One for the dreadlocks, as long as they didn't smoke ganja inside. They didn't consider this a problem and simply went into the garden. Coxsone built a fence around the grass, hoping not to attract much attention. After all, smoking the herb was and still is illegal in Jamaica. The Rasta musicians introduced their African hand drum style, using bongos and congas, combined with a tighter form of drumming. Count Ossie was one of them.

With the rise of the black power movement in the USA, closely followed by the Jamaican population, song texts more often dealt with social injustices and protests. The black part of the nation grew more conscious about the actual situation in the country and stopped taking it for granted. Reggae proved to be an excellent vehicle in spreading that protest message. By the way, contrary to the rude boys, the Rastafarians oppose violence and mainly preach love and tolerance.

When Perry Henzell's classic *The Harder They Come* was released in 1972, with Jimmy Cliff loosely impersonating Rude Boy Ivanhoe "Rhyging" Martin, it meant a huge international impulse for Jamaican music in general and reggae particularly. Given the soundtrack with songs of Cliff, Toots & the Maytals and Desmond Dekker, it came as no surprise. The latter musician is often mentioned as the singer who released the first reggae song ever, "Israelites", in 1968. However, the careful listener might pick up strong ska influences in this tune.

In 1973 Chris Blackwell produced the first Wailers album *Catch a Fire* with which reggae started its unstoppable march to conquer the world. How Blackwell and the Wailers got in touch and why the record boss felt connected to the Rastafarians is a story in itself worth exploring.

Chris Blackwell was born out of a marriage between Irishman Middleton Joseph Blackwell and Jamaican Blanche Lindo, a descendant of Portuguese Sephardic Jews. She was a very colourful character and years after her divorce from Chris' father had a long love affair with Ian Fleming, the literary father of James Bond. There is even a small airfield on Jamaica named after the author. Blanche was his muse and probably a role model for Pussy Galore in the story *Goldfinger.*

The Lindo family had made their fortune on the island with sugar and Appleton rum. Chris was sent to Great Britain for his further education. University didn't appeal to him and he returned to his birth grounds, where he became the personal assistant of Sir Hugh Foot, at the time governor of Jamaica. Chris wanted a more adventurous life and pursued a career as real estate agent cum jukebox manager. The job brought him all over the island and connected him to the Jamaican musical society.

When his sailboat ran aground in 1958 on a coral reef near Hellshire Beach, he swam to the coast for help. The intense heat exhausted him, whereupon he crashed on the beach, seriously wounded. He was found by a small group of Rasta fishermen who took him to their huts, cared for his injuries and fed him their traditional food.

This accident caused Blackwell to become intricately connected to the Jamaican culture, the music and the Rastas. The same year, only 22 years old, Blackwell founded his first record company, backed financially by his parents, and named it Island.

It took him one year before he got his first hit single with the ska tune "Boogy in my Bones" by Laurel Aitkin, aka the Godfather of Ska. When Blackwell moved his company to London in 1962, Island went crescendo, rapidly becoming one of the most successful independent record companies.

Blackwell signed some of music's greats: Cat Stevens, The Cranberries, Emerson, Lake & Palmer, The Free, Grace Jones, Jethro Tull, Roxy Music and Tom Waits. In the decade to come he focused on rock and pop music, leaving Jamaican music on its own. That attitude changed when he met Bob Marley in 1972 when Bob ran aground in London, penniless. Blackwell offered The Wailers an opportunity to record what would eventually become the *Catch A Fire* album. They never signed a contract for it. The successful record producer advised Bob Marley to slightly develop his reggae in the direction of rock music. From that moment on the group was named Bob Marley & The Wailers.

Blackwell had a nose for talent and in later years would contract Melissa Etheridge and U2, among others. He did make a few mistakes, for instance with Elton John, whom he considered "too shy" to perform. Well, you win some, you lose some!

The winners were Bob and Chris. The story of Blackwell and Marley is a beautiful example of conceptual continuity. Once the forefathers of Blackwell's mother Blanche earned a fortune with rum and sugar, over the backs of "imported" slaves from Africa. At a young age Blackwell was saved by Rasta fishermen. He eventually founded his record company Island thanks to the rum fortune made by those forefathers and now, in 1973 he offered a group of Rastafarian musicians the opportunity to record a reggae album with no contract at all. That album now is one of the all time classics in this genre. For me this is where rum & reggae come full circle in this book and why I chose the title.

Jamaica would not have been Jamaica if the music didn't progress beyond reggae. Producers Lee Perry and King Tubby dedicated themselves to making "version singles" – basically a different mix of an existing song. This development led to the release of dub albums on which one particular song was repeated extensively, each time in a different re-mix.

The Wailers, until then merely a vocal harmony group on reggae riddims, gradually transformed into a rock band with a form of reggae appealing to the masses. Bob Marley, in the mean time converted to the Rasta way of life due to the influence of his wife Rita and his mentor Mortimer Planno, became not only a billboard for this religious movement, but also for the Jamaican government. The latter saw no harm in billing the dreadlocks they had despised not a decade earlier as the cultural heritage of the nation. Nothing like opportunism in politics.

Reggae, in short, became cultural music. In the UK the punkers felt kinship with the "sufferahs" in the ghettos of Kingston, which culminated in a temporary love affair between both genres. Soon punk had to disconnect. Not only because of its musical poorness, but mainly because the Rasta ideas and the punk ideals weren't exactly seamlessly integrated. As a punker you might want to wear dreadlocks and puff up a joint, but propagating the One Love message of Ras Tafari, abstinence from alcohol and converting to vegetarianism is a different cup of tea. No Punky Reggae Party will permanently cross that bridge.

When in 1975 Burning Spear launched his seminal reggae album *Marcus Garvey* in the UK, the Rastafarian movement took a huge international jump. To better understand the relationship between reggae and Rasta it is useful to delve a bit deeper into the history and the rituals of the movement itself. Let's travel back to the end of the 19th century.

***

The Rastafari Movement

Marcus Garvey is considered by many as the father of Rasta. He was born in Jamaica on August 17, 1887 and developed into a political and religious leader whose favourite themes were Black Nationalism and Pan Africanism. He preached the return of the African Diaspora to their countries of origin. A Roman Catholic, Garvey was a gifted speaker, entrepreneur, publisher and journalist, whose talents helped him to widely spread his ideas. For this purpose he founded the Universal Negro Improvement Association and African Communities League, in short UNIA-ACL. To further support his back-to-Africa philosophy he established a ship company called Black Star Line. People could book their passage to Africa on his ships.

Garvey is credited with proclaiming "Look to Africa, when a black king shall be crowned, for the day of deliverance is at hand!" possibly referring to the return of Jesus Christ. When Haile Selassie, whose real name was Ras Tafari Makonnen, was crowned emperor of Ethiopia in 1930, Garvey's words were considered a prophesy. Over time the question has arisen whether he was the source of this quote, since no written evidence can be found. What does exist is a book written by his contemporary and associate Rev. James Morris Web, which was published in 1919, titled *A Black Man Will Be the Coming Universal King, Proven by Biblical History*.

Haile Selassie claimed direct decadency from King Solomon and the Queen of Sheba. Various Bible texts, among others in the book of Genesis, have been interpreted to mean that the second coming of Jesus Christ would take place in Africa, birthplace of *Homo sapiens*. The complexity of those texts is that they lend themselves to more than one interpretation. Anyway, the name Rastafari is derived from the former Ethiopian emperor, who is considered by many Rastas as God's substitute on earth. Garvey later distanced himself from Selassie.

Although the Rastafarians are monotheistic in principle, their ideas have been influenced by ancient religious traditions brought from Africa. The Rastas are convinced they descend from one of Israel's twelve tribes, outcast to Africa, meaning Ethiopia, which name is their synonym for heaven. They call it Zion and believe Jah (God) promised them those lands. No other heaven exists for them, neither does death. Many reggae songs refer to Zion. Rastas consider their body a temple of God and in this way can worship Him wherever they want. They do not necessarily see the Rastafari movement as an organized form of religion or outlook on life.

The movement does recognise three main streams: the Nyabinghi Order, the Bobo Ashanti and the Twelve Tribes of Israel. Bob Marley joined the last. They differ in details and in their regulations one can find many Old Testament Jewish customs regarding food, drink and personal hygiene. Many Rastas do not belong to any order at all.

A fourth order was founded by Leonard Howell in 1932 – officially named The Rastafari Movement. He lived with his disciples in the so-called Pinnacle Settlement and they were constantly attacked. More than once Howell disappeared behind bars. That might have been either prison or an asylum. In his main work *The Promise Key* he did not preach the typical Rasta conviction that all men are equal. On the contrary, in his view the black race was superior and should take revenge for the white people's wickedness.

Howell also recognized Haile Selassie as the only true king of all the black peoples. With this attitude he ran into trouble with the government since Jamaica was a British colony at the time. His refusal to acknowledge Great Britain's monarch made him a prey for the powers that be. Howell is sometimes called the First Rasta, although he never wore dreadlocks – the outer distinguishing feature among many Rastas.

Dreadlocks

The long intertwined strands of hair are inextricably connected to reggae and Rastas. They call Western society Babylon, to them a synonym for everything that is evil in their eyes. Comb, scissors and razor are Babylonian artefacts. Apart from that, the growing of their hair symbolises freedom with no ties. The dreadlocks also represent the manes of the Lion of Judah, symbol for the eponymous tribe from the Old Testament, but also a representation of Jesus Christ, who is called Lion of Judah in the book of Revelation. Readers familiar with C.S. Lewis's work *The Chronicles of Narnia* might recall the lion Aslan as a metaphor for Christ (Aslan is Turkish for lion). The Rastafarians furthermore point at Samson, who wore his hair in seven locks, a holy number. When Delilah cut his hair while he was asleep, he lost his powers.

Many reggae musicians wear such hairdos and are therefore called dreadlocks or natty dreads. Not all Rastas do. After all they are tolerant and peace minded, leaving ample room for the individual to create his own outlook on life. Bob Marley reputedly said one time: "Not every dreadlock is a Rasta, and not every Rasta is a dreadlock."

Ceremonies

The Rastas perform two important ceremonies, Reasoning and Grounation. The former is a kind of meeting to discuss matters under the influence of ganja. The one who lights the joint says a short prayer after which it is passed around clockwise. In wartime, counter-clockwise.

Ganja, considered a holy herb, enlightens the mind, so the discussion can follow broader paths and one can reason with Jah. Facts do not exist in the world of the Rastas – and some say even in Jamaica – so people are encouraged to a free association of thoughts. Many years ago I tried it myself, with a group of friends, taping it on a cassette recorder. Under the influence we were convinced to have uttered extreme pearls of wisdom and insight. Listening to the tape the next morning was revealing and sobering. From the speakers a murky brew of words, mumblings and the like sounded in the room, interlaced with cries like "Yea man, really man, I dig this, man." The tape did not reveal what was so real and dug. One can only hope the Rastas reach far deeper insights.

The other ceremony is also called *binghi*, derived from the African word Nyabinghi, the name of an ancient extinct tribe that battled against suppression. Binghis often take up a number of days, during which vast amounts of ganja are smoked, with singing, dancing and partying. Throughout the year certain fixed grounations are held, one of which, April 21, is officially called Grounation Day. On that date in the year 1966 Haile Selassie paid a visit to Jamaica and was welcomed by so many people that he could only leave the plane after many hours, with the help of Rasta leader Mortimer Planno. His arrival was filmed for posterity and available on YouTube: http://www.youtube.com/watch?v=8rZlVkBwgpg.

Smoking cannabis or possessing the herb is illegal in most parts of the world, Jamaica included. The Rastas however see the smoking of ganja as a sacrament and refer to a whole plethora of Bible texts, allegedly supporting the use of cannabis on religious grounds. One who wants to try this argument when caught might find wisdom and a way out in Genesis 1:11, 1:29, 3:18, Psalm 104:14, Proverbs 15:17 and Revelation 22:2.

The etymology of the word cannabis might be found in the Holy Scriptures, too. Some scholars claim the roots are in the Hebrew *qaneh bosm*, an herb which the Lord presents to Moses in Exodus 30:23, to produce a holy, aromatic oil. A legend maintains that cannabis was the first herb growing on king Solomon's grave. Well, all the more reason to always carry your Bible with you. But let's be clear about this, I do not guarantee anything.

Various court cases have been held regarding the legalisation of cannabis on religious grounds, usually not to the advantage of the herb's proponents. Cannabis, by the way, probably came to Jamaica via migrants from India, who flooded the island in the early part of the 20th century, looking for work.

Language

The Rastas consider the English language forced by the colonial oppressor upon their ancestors, who would have spoken Amharic (at least in Ethiopia). As a result they lost their own language. Hence they developed a specific dialect known as lyaric. English words and expressions are somewhat changed. Bredren (brethren) and sistern (sister) become idrin; dedication becomes livication, since the Rastas phonetically associate that word with death, a state they do not acknowledge. The plural "we" is not used. Instead the Rasta says "I and I", emphasising the fact that everybody is an individual. The term Rastafarianism is not to their liking since in their worldview, facts and dogmas do not exist, hence no –isms! Respecting their opinion I tried to avoid using it while writing this book. Lyaric brings us back to reggae itself. Many of these created words return in lyrics and song titles, such as "Hail Me Idrin" by Ini Kamoze.

***

Just before we took off exploring Rasta culture, we were rummaging around in 1975, a year marking the big UK breakthrough of Bob Marley and the Wailers, with concerts that led to the famed *Live* album. By then, both other original Wailers had left the group to go their own way. Bob Marley, the slender young man with the dreadlocks and piercing eyes not only is a rock star, but a public figure with (unwanted) political influence, whose messages resound on an international stage. He is credited with messianic powers, partly based on stories from his youth, a time in which he was rumoured to have exercised supernatural and prophetic powers.

Reggae has turned into a message and the musical style is adopted throughout the world by bands known and unknown. Even the Fathers of Hardrock, Led Zeppelin, dare to record a reggae song. Listen to "D'yer Mak'er" (phonetic wordplay on Jamaica), from the *Houses of the Holy* album (http://www.youtube.com/watch?v=P5s9illHQlc). Cover band Dread Zeppelin specialises in reggae versions of popular hard rock songs. Even the Rolling Stones went natty dread. Keith Richards purchased a house on the island, where Mick Jagger and Peter Tosh jammed "Walk" and "Don't Look Back" (http://www.youtube.com/watch?v=3o4Fgh0KW_4). 10CC released the legendary *Bloody Tourists* album with evergreen "Dreadlock Holiday" (http://www.youtube.com/watch?v=Vk7axzWWw80). When Eric Clapton adapted "I Shot the Sheriff" (http://www.youtube.com/watch?v=10qLYy6hiFQ), covering the song on his *461 Ocean Boulevard* album, Marley turned into a living legend. Outside Jamaica, Bob Marley is a super hero and even in the tiniest village "No Woman No Cry" can be heard.

1975 also marked the rise of Jamaica's most famous rhythm tandem and producers duo – Sly Dunbar and Robbie Shakespeare. In the years to follow they left an indelible stamp on the development of reggae and musical forms derived from it.

In the mean time the violence between rude boys, organized in gangs led by bodyguards, previous employees of the Sound System bosses, continued and culminated in the Green Bay Massacre of 1978, during which five alleged JLP-supporters were killed. Then, the gangs had enough, so it seemed. Rivalling gang leaders Claudie Massop and Bucky Marshall tracked down Bob Marley in London and convinced him to come back to Jamaica. He was supposed to perform on April 22 at the *One Love Peace Concert* in Kingston, which was billed as a musical truce. Bob accepted and returned, only to be shot by a small gang of rude boys who begged to differ. He miraculously survived and even performed.

He managed to get the rivalling leaders of the PNP and JLP, respectively Michael Manley and Edward Seaga, to come on stage and shake hands. Reggae, Bob Marley's reggae that is, had become an instrument in the realm of international politics. That same year Bob was rewarded for his action and received the United Nations Peace Medal. A world tour to bring reggae to all corners of the world followed the next year. The band even appeared in Japan and

Down Under, and was scheduled for four concerts in Africa. One of them was to take place in Zimbabwe, celebrating its state of independence. When Marley discovered there was no money available, he personally financed the trip with $250,000, buying airline tickets, lodging and food for the whole crew.

Europe also heard his universal message that Ras Tafari is the human embodiment of God, that mankind should unite in love and smoking ganja should be legalised worldwide. That message, or part thereof, is not without consequences. Witness the tolerant "coffee shop view" in the Netherlands.

Reggae was at its peak, but Bob Marley started going downhill, rapidly. When jogging in Central Park, NYC in 1980 he suddenly collapsed and was taken to a hospital by a friend. The doctors discovered a malign cancer growth, probably related to his cancer of three years earlier, metastasised in lungs and liver. Marley gathered the strength to perform in Pittsburgh, Pennsylvania later that year. Sadly it proved to be his swan song. Close to the year end he flew to a specialised clinic in southern Germany for treatment by a German doctor using obscure methods. Herr Doktor managed to keep the slender musician alive for some months but told him in May 1981 he had run out of options. Marley wanted to die in Jamaica and flew back, only reaching Miami, where he passed away on May 11, in his mother's house, surrounded by family.

Edward Seaga, the former anthropologist, music producer and (political) advocate, had just been chosen as

WELCOME
TO
NINE MILES
DRIVE WITH CARE
WE LOVE OUR CHILDREN
CARTER'S ENTERPRISE

Prime Minister. He arranged a state funeral and gave the eulogy himself. Bob Marley's body was taken to his birthplace Nine Miles in St Ann's parish. His former house on 56 Hope Road in Kingston has been converted into the Bob Marley Museum. Posthumously he was honoured with a statue and his portrait has been printed on a series of Jamaican stamps.

Reggae lives on in more than his image. Marley's children, quite a collection he fathered with different women, received his musical heritage. His sons Ziggy, Julian, Stephen and Damian continue to build on their father's musical foundation, each adding a unique, personal flavour to it. Bob's official wife and widow Rita, continues to record music and has played an important role in keeping his legacy alive. In line with the Rasta worldview she opens her house to all Bob's children, regardless with whom they were conceived.

Bob was the first of the original Wailers to die. Peter Tosh followed in 1987, shot in his own house by a gang of rude boys who demanded money he didn't possess. Six years earlier Bob Marley confided on his death bed to his son Ziggy, "Money can't buy life." Bunny Livingston, preferring to be called Bunny Wailer, continues to perform, and has recorded many albums over the decades.

The I-Threes were vocal support of Bob Marley & The Wailers. Rita Marley was joined by Judy Mowatt and Marcia Griffiths, who all are alive to date and built successful solo careers. Judy Mowatt, originally coming from the musical Gaylettes trio, used to be the figurehead of women in Rasta, until she converted to Christianity. She lost her dreadlocks but not her voice, singing for Jesus instead of Jah, primarily at gospel shows.

When Marcia Griffiths joined the I-Threes she was a star in her own right. In 1970 she scored a huge hit with the song "Young, Gifted and Black". The record still sells, but according to Marcia she never got a penny. It appears she is not too annoyed about that: "Music has to live, it is not only about money, but about the satisfaction I get with work I love. That's why I go for it, every day." She carries her given title the Empress of Reggae with grace and still performs on a global scale.

Reggae's musical origin is difficult to trace. Most probably the trail leads back to the blues, father of all popular music, with deep, deep roots in African music and culture. The blues platform witnessed so many launches of variations on the theme, like jazz, soul, calypso, zydeco, Cajun, R&B, who all, in their own way contributed to mento, ska and rocksteady, culminating in reggae.

Where reggae stops is equally difficult to determine. Roots reggae as played by Bob Marley is performed worldwide by many bands, some of them led by one of his children. Reggae sprouted into different directions such as Lovers Rock, a romantic version blooming in Great Britain, counteracting the militant roots songs. American soul songs were a rich soil for reggaed cover versions. Roots reggae, back to basics, with the emphasis on the life of the sufferahs in the ghettos of Kingston, is personified these days by Jephter McClymont performing as Luciano.

Dancehall is a development from the early 1980s. Evolution in electronics made it possible to produce an infinite number of mixes and the instrumentation was largely computerised. Singers and DJs sing-speak over previously programmed rhythms. This illustrates the big difference with the original Jamaican dancehall music played by the Sound Systems some decades earlier. Ragga takes it a step further and exclusively uses digital instruments.

Dub, briefly addressed previously, morphed over time into hip hop and rap. The current rap generation has to pay honour to Count Matchuki, Scratch Perry and King Tubby, who laid a solid foundation for rap at the turn of the 1950s.

Linton Kwesi Johnson may without doubt be named the icon of reggae poetry. The British musician turned toasting into an art itself. Born in Jamaica in 1952, he left for Great Britain at a young age. He became successful when he started to declare his poems over reggae music. LKJ is politically engaged and his texts usually treat social injustice. He sing-speaks with a Jamaican-English accent.

The framework of this book leaves no room to mention all existing reggae derivatives. The music blew to the four corners of the world and came to rest not only in Great Britain but also gained strongholds in Africa, Australia and the USA. Reggae keeps rediscovering, reinventing and mutating itself.

I have a preference for roots reggae. With a glass of rum at hand I enjoy listening to Peter Tosh, Bob Marley, Black Uhuru, Eddy Grant or LKJ. The chapter Listening

Guide presents some of my favourite tracks. What rum should accompany those songs? I gladly leave that to the reader. The more tastes, the more preferences. And... those who would rather go for hip hop or rap... it's just a different brew.

In July 2012 world-famous rapper Snoop Dogg made a remarkable announcement after he had met a Rasta priest in Jamaica. At a press conference in NYC he remarked along these lines: "He asked my name. I said 'Snoop Dogg'. He looked me in the eye and said: 'No more. You are the light, you are the lion.' Then I understood why I was there." Snoop Dogg added that from then on he would be known as Snoop Lion and his next recording would be a reggae album. "Then my grandma can listen to my songs, too." In short, he felt a reborn Rasta.

Enjoy a good glass of rum in the company of timeless music and toast to Count Matchuki, Lee Perry, King Tubby or Bob Marley.

Yo mon', see ya on The Road, come soon.

LISTENING GUIDE

Listening Guide

The following songs and albums are in my list of favourites. Without intentional neglect of other fantastic musicians, I will limit myself to a selection from my collection. After all it is a matter of taste, similar to what rum you'd like to choose with which song. Let the reader be the judge of that.

One of my favourite rums is the 12-year-old expression of Appleton. A dram I could savour each and every day. And when I listen to Eddy Grant I will probably pour Demerara rum, both subjects coming from Guyana.

Enjoy the sound, the images, combined with the aromas and flavours of the rum you choose. What follows is a list. Not chronologically, but alphabetically. Take your pick.

Black Uhuru – "Sponji Reggae"
To be enjoyed live. Captured in Glastonbury, 1982. The original version can be found on the album *Red* (1981), with the super line-up Michael Rose, Puma Jones and Ducky Simpson, supported by one of the world's greatest rhythm duos: Sly Dunbar and Robbie Shakespeare.

http://www.youtube.com/watch?v=AYUtEMf0fFQ

Bunny Wailer – "Armagideon"
Neville O'Riley Livingston, aka Bunny Wailer and Jah B is

the only original Wailer still alive and performing. Lately at Sumfest 2012 in Montego Bay, at dawn, when the sun rose out of the Caribbean. This one is from his first solo album *Blackheart Man*, 1976, with none other than Robbie Shakespeare:

http://www.youtube.com/watch?v=A_E8MXYj8FQ

Sit back and relax if you are in for an entire concert from Madison Square Garden (1986). Bunny leads the show, dressed like a sort of high priest. Mixed with archive material, among others footage of Haile Selassie:

http://www.youtube.com/watch?v=V30zPF7YH7o

Burning Spear – *Marcus Garvey*
This album was released in 1975 and regarded as a milestone in reggae music. Below a reference to a more recent recording with a lot of swing:

http://www.youtube.com/watch?v=XWv_e-xGQkY

Cliff, Jimmy – *The Harder They Come*
This 1972 movie meant a great deal for the rise of reggae. Jamaican musician Jimmy Cliff had made a name for himself when asked to play the main part. The clip is a promo for the entire movie, a must see.

http://www.youtube.com/watch?v=xGE4dnrPPZQ

Dekker, Desmond – "Israelites"
Often named the first real reggae song. However the transformation of mento via ska and rocksteady into reggae was a gradual one. This classic cannot be left out in this guide. Listen to the clear ska, mento and even calypso influences:

http://www.youtube.com/watch?v=r5JHGi0awgc&playnext=1&list=PLE119553B0E623886&feature=results_main

Franklin, Aretha – "Rock Steady"
Beautifully sung by a young Aretha Franklin, recorded on the *Young, Gifted and Black* album from 1971. It's soul, funk, rocksteady, ska and reggae at the same time. A true melting pot of styles.

http://www.youtube.com/watch?v=wmOX_Ll1Txb8

No? Try this one, you get another chance:

http://www.youtube.com/watch?v=EiB8_PpWedk

....Funky reggae party, yeah!

Grant, Eddy – "Living on the Front Line"
Honour him with a glass of Demerara rum in hand. Guyana musician and dram. I prefer the 1981 version from *Live at Notting Hill*, but this concert is also one to be enjoyed:

http://www.youtube.com/watch?v=v4ETVsQoCLw

Johnson, Linton Kwesi – "Want Fi Go Rave"

From the *Forces of Victory* album, 1979. By far my favourite reggae record. Made for a lazy, warm late summer evening on the veranda. Just play the entire album. Contemplate gently about the world. Do you get up for another glass of Appleton Reserve, or keep your seat? Here is the original first:

http://www.youtube.com/watch?v=nqx9ElThn3M

The next one is a recording from 2012 at the *Back to Black Festival*. LKJ plays "Rave", which segues into the powerful "Sonny's Lettah", also originally recorded on *Forces*:
http://www.youtube.com/watch?v=0snHbj7XhrI

Kamoze, Ini – "Trouble You a Trouble Me"

Taken from his debut album *Ini Kamoze*, 1984. Incredibly clear voice and ditto sound. A song that makes me happy. Can't sit still:

http://www.youtube.com/watch?v=32Eqg98vR4k

Marley, Bob – "Simmer Down"

His first hit on Jamaica was a ska song in which a very young Bob Marley begged the rude boys of Kingston to take it easy. Tosh, Bunny and Bob then looked quite different, as the album cover reveals:

http://www.youtube.com/watch?v=ybmPHD7FPcQ

Marley, Bob – "Stir it Up"
Especially enjoy it from the *Babylon by Bus* recording from 1978. The clip below shows the first ever recording with the Wailers, taken at the BBC studios in 1973. It's much slower and the guitar makes that typical "chka" sound from where the term ska is derived:

http://www.youtube.com/watch?v=n6U-TGahwvs

Marley, Bob – "No Woman, No Cry"
I'm a sucker for the *Live* album version of 1975. The ultimate reggae song in my humble opinion. At the tender age of 19 I first heard the entire record at a girlfriend's place and could not run quickly enough to the record shop next morning to obtain my own copy.

Below is a reference to a seven minute live recording from 1979, in which the evolution of the tune can be heard so well. An epic song:
http://www.youtube.com/watch?v=jGqrvn3q1oo

Marley, Damian – *Live*
This is how Damian approaches his father's musical legacy, an hour of live recordings. The Marley brothers testify to the fact they have taken their father's work to heart, pursuing active careers in music. As far as I'm concerned Ziggy (1968), Stephen (1972), Julian (1975) and Damian (1978) must continue on the road taken for a long time.

http://www.youtube.com/watch?v=HT2789urycI

Marley, Julian – "Lion in the Morning"
A recording from 2011, during the *Live Africa* concert, presents Julian's interpretation of his father's music:

http://www.youtube.com/watch?v=deKzONAlba0

Marley, Stephen – "Woman I Love"
This incredibly beautiful song is part of his first album, *Mind Control* from 2007:

http://www.youtube.com/watch?v=m1mJpuKvULk&feature=related

**Marley, Ziggy and The Melody Makers –
"Tomorrow People"**
For a romantic mood. It's such a soft and friendly song, it almost makes you cry from warmth and happiness. The clip shows Ziggy Marley, eerily resembling his father:

http://www.youtube.com/watch?v=AM8M-HHSbp0

**Prince Buster –
"Madness" and "One Step Beyond"**
One of the Big Sound System Operators sang, too. Both songs are classical forerunners of reggae with clear ska influences. Here's some "Madness":

http://www.youtube.com/watch?v=EZC6Ot1MLP0

Buster also composed the song "One Step Beyond", which would become a giant hit during the British ska revival of the late 1970s and early 1980s, performed by a group who named themselves after Buster's other song. First listen to the Man:

http://www.youtube.com/watch?v=D3DAHAPLaVI

And then as expressed by the British band Madness, from 1979:
http://www.youtube.com/watch?v=N-uyWAe0NhQ

The Skatalites – "Guns of Navarone"
A ska song originally released in 1968, which survived time. This is a recording from the 1990s in a jazzy framework with a tight offbeat. The horn section is incredible:

http://www.youtube.com/watch?v=5PBNawAPdss

This was the first Jamaican super group and "Guns of Navarone" was composed in 1964. The Skatalites were highly influential on the development of reggae, collectively as well as individually. That's why I state their names below, with some added musicians, who would sometimes join in at recording sessions:

Don Drummond - trombone
Jackie Mittoo – piano
Jerome "Jah Jerry" Haynes - guitar

Johnny "Dizzy" Moore - trumpet
Lester Sterling - alto saxophone
Lloyd Brevett - upright bass
Lloyd Knibbs – drums
Roland Alphonso - tenor saxophone
Tommy McCook - tenor saxophone, flute
+
Dennis "Ska" Campbell - tenor saxophone
Doreen Shaeffer - vocals
Ernest Ranglin - lead guitar
Frank Anderson - trumpet
Jackie Opel - vocals
Lord Tanamo - vocals
Lyn Taitt - rhythm guitar
Oswald "Baba" Brooks – trumpet
Tony Gregory - vocals

Cleopatra Records launched a compilation of *100 Reggae and Ska Hits* in 2010/2011. On it is an early version from Roland Alphonso and The Skatalites.

Steel Pulse – "Steppin' Out"
Another gem. One of the British answers to Jamaican reggae surprised the musical world in 1978 with their debut album *Handsworth Revolution*. The version below is from a concert in Colorado, 2008. Nice heavy guitar intro, vaguely reminds me of Steve Vai:

http://www.youtube.com/watch?v=pTI1FaHf9U4&feature=related

Toots & The Maytals – "Reggae Got Soul"
The man who is the self-proclaimed inventor of the word
reggae cannot be left out. Listen to the clear influences of
American soul music. Toots has passed the 65 year thresh-
old but his voice has not lost its power. The original version is from 1976, from the eponymous album. You might
pick up a bit of Otis Redding flavour here:

http://www.youtube.com/watch?v=IqgcO5V_snY

Tosh, Peter – "Johnny Be Good"
Gooseflesh-inspiring music at its best. Listen to the Steppin Razor's reggae version of Chuck Berry's old rock 'n'
roll hit. The clip shows Tosh's favourite pastime – mono-
cycling. The song can also be found on the *Gold Collection*,
a compilation launched in 1996. This is one of my all time
favourites:

http://www.youtube.com/watch?v=q8WRzdN43BI

UB 40 – "Food for Thought"
Taken from their first album *Signing Off*, released in 1980.
Riding on the ska revival, UB 40 started out as a group of
friends who shared being unemployed. The name comes
from a form that had to be filled out when out of work:
Unemployment Benefit Form 40. They conquered the
world with their attractive mix of danceable ska, reggae
and pop music. Their first to me is still their best.

Here is the original from 1980:

http://www.youtube.com/watch?v=58ZiayUPn_Y

Still very popular in 2012, as can be seen and heard on this recent recording in Paradiso, Amsterdam. The sound quality isn't great and in the course of 32 years there is hardly any progress in song nor musicians, but nostalgia made me include this one:

http://www.youtube.com/watch?v=0TBFCSro6Eo

U-Roy – "True Born African"
From 2010. What a deep, deep voice, what charisma !

http://www.youtube.com/watch?v=q_8AAdV76jo

I could go on like this but I have to offer some rum suggestions now. Browse through the list on the following pages. You will find more than 170 variations. One and hopefully more of them will surely be to your liking.

RUM GUIDE

Rum Listed by Brand

Brand	*Country*
10Cane	Trinidad & Tobago
Abuelo	Panama
Admiral Nelson	British Virgin Islands
Admiral Rodney	St. Lucia
Alma de Bohemia	Dominican Republic
Angostura	Trinidad & Tobago
Appleton	Jamaica
Arehucas	Spain
Artemi	Canary Islands
Asmussen	Germany (Jamaica)
Atlantico	Dominican Republic
Arecha	Cuba
Bacardi	Jamaica, Puerto Rico, St. Croix
Banks	Caribbean
Baquba	Trinidad & Tobago
Barbancourt	Haïti
Barcelo	Dominican Republic
Bearhug	Barbados
Belmont Estate	St. Kitts & Nevis
Bermudez	Dominican Republic
Blackbeard	Puerto Rico
Black Cat	Suriname
Blackheart	Puerto Rico
Black Seal	Bermuda
Blackwell	Jamaica
Blossa Glögg + Rum	Denmark

Brand	Country
Bombardino Roner	Italy
Boote Star	Guyana
Borgoe	Suriname
Botran	Guatemala
Bounty	St. Lucia
Brinley	St. Kitts
Brugal	Dominican Republic
Bundaberg	Australia
Cadenhead	Barbados, Guyana, Jamaica
Calavera 1492	Dominican Republic
Caliche	Puerto Rico
Cana de Belem (cachaça)	Brazil
Caney	Cuba
Capitan Kidd	Canary Islands
Captain Marley	Spain
Captain Morgan	Jamaica, Puerto Rico, St. Croix
Caribaya	US Virgin Islands
Cartavio	Peru
Centenario	Costa Rica
Chairman's Reserve	St. Lucia
Christal	Ecuador
Ciguena Carta	Barbados (Dutch market)
Clement	Martinique
Cockspur	Barbados
Comandante Fidel	Cuba
Conch Knockemdown	USA
Conde de Cuba	Dominican Republic
Coruba	Jamaica

Brand	**Country**
Cruzan	St. Croix, US Virgin Islands
Damoiseau	Guadeloupe
De Caldas	Colombia
De Kuyper Rum Punch	Jamaica (Dutch market)
Denizen	Jamaica/Trinidad
Depaz	Martinique
Dictador	Colombia
Dillon	Martinique
Dominican Club	Dominican Republic
Don Q	Puerto Rico
Don Rhon	Dominican Republic
Dos Ron	Dominican Republic (German market)
Doorly's	Barbados
Duquesne	Martinique
Dzama	Madagascar
E.S.A. Field	Barbados
Edmundo Dantes	Cuba
El Dorado	Guyana
Elements	St. Lucia
English Harbour	Antigua
Estaro	The Netherlands
Estelar	Ecuador
Flor de Cana	Nicaragua
Freihof Jagertee	Austria

Brand	**Country**
Golden Ganja	Germany
Gosling	Bermuda
Guajiro	Canary Islands
Harpoon	Jamaica
Havana Club	Cuba, Jamaica, Puerto Rico, St. Croix
Hemingway	Colombia
Holy Dollar	Australia
HSE	St. Etienne
Inner Circle	Australia
Isautier	Reunion
Isla N	Argentina
J.M.	Martinique
Jack Tarr	Guyana, Jamaica (South African market)
Jäger Inlander	Austria
Jeffersons 1785	Caribbean
John D. Taylor	Barbados
Jolly Roger	US Virgin Islands
Jumbie	Caribbean
Kaniche	Barbados
Karukera	Guadeloupe
Koko Kanu	Jamaica
Kraken	Trinidad & Tobago

Brand	**Country**
La Buse	Reunion
La Favorite	Martinique
La Mauny	Martinique
Lambs Navy Rum	Barbados
Leblon (cachaça)	Brazil
Lemon Hart	Guyana
Long Pond	Jamaica
Malecon	Panama
Malibu	Barbados
Malteco	Guatemala
Matusalem	Dominican Republic
Martí Mojito Rum	Caribbean
Medellin	Colombia
Millonario	Peru
Mocambo	Mexico
Mombacho	Nicaragua
Montebello	Guadeloupe
Montego	Caribbean
Mount Gay	Barbados
Musee du Rhum Coeur Chauffe	Guadeloupe
Myers's	Jamaica
Nassau Royale Liqueur	Bahamas
Negrita	France
Neisson	Martinique
New Grove	Mauritius
No. 1	Sweden

Brand	Country
Old Captain	Jamaica
Old Jamaica	Jamaica
Old Monk	India
Old Port	India
Old Vatted Demerara	Guyana
One Barrel	Belize
Oronoco	Brazil
Papagayo	Paraguay
Père Labat	Marie-Galante
Pink Pigeon	Mauritius
Pitú (cachaça)	Brazil
Plantage Cane Rhum	Caribbean
Plantation	Jamaica, Grenada, Guyana, Nicaragua, St. Lucia, Trinidad & Tobago
Port Mourant	Guyana
Pott	Jamaica (German market)
Prichard's	USA
Punta Cana	Colombia
Pusser's	British Virgin Islands
Pyrat	Anguilla
Rancado	India
Renegade	Brazil, Guadeloupe, Guyana, Jamaica
Riviere du Mat	Reunion
Ron de Jeremy	Panama
Ron Llave	Puerto Rico

Rum Guide

Brand	Country
Ronrico	Puerto Rico
Roquez	Reunion
Rum Bar	Jamaica
Sagatiba (cachaça)	Brazil
Sailor Jerry	St. Croix, US Virgin Islands
Saint James	Martinique
Sangster's	Jamaica
Savanna	Reunion
Sea Wynde	Jamaica
Seven Tiki	Fiji Islands
Sikkim	India
Smith & Cross	Jamaica
Spicy Gold	Caribbean
Stroh	Austria
St. Lucia	St. Lucia
Takamaka Bay	Seychelles
Tanduay	Philippines
Tiburon	Aruba
Tondena	Philippines
TOZ	St. Lucia
Trois Rivieres	Martinique
Tunel	Mallorca
Turoa	Germany
Ultimatum	
Summum & Infinitum	Barbados, Guyana, Jamaica, Trinidad, (Dutch market)

Brand	Country
Vana Tallin	Estonia
Virgin Gorda	British Virgin Islands
Vizcaya	Caribbean
Westindien Ubersee	British Virgin Islands
White Diamond	Mauritius
Worthy Gold	Jamaica
Wray & Nephew	Jamaica
Xtabentun	Mexico
Ypioca (cachaça)	Brazil
Zacapa	Guatemala
Zafra	Panama
Zapatera	Nicaragua
Zuidam Flying Dutchman	The Netherlands

A rum guide is never complete, since so many rums have been bottled under private label, a custom that has held sway for centuries. Therefore you may not find all your favourites in this guide. The label above is a beautiful example of a private bottling from Charleston, South Carolina. Note the list of cocktails, old and new.

Rum Listed by Country

Country	*Brand*
Anguilla	Pyrat
Antigua	English Harbour, Sailor Jerry
Argentina	Isla N
Aruba	Tiburon
Australia	Bundaberg, Holy Dollar, Inner Circle
Austria	Freihof Jagertee, Jäger Inlander, Stroh
Bahamas	Nassau Royale Liqueur
Barbados	Bearhug, Cadenhead, Ciguene Carta, Cockspur, Doorly's, E.S.A. Field, Foursquare, John D. Taylor, Kaniche, Lambs Navy Rum, Malibu, Mount Gay
Belize	One Barrel
Bermuda	Black Seal, Gosling's Family Reserve
Brazil	Cana de Belem, Leblon, Pitú, Sagatiba, Ypioca (cachaça); Oronoco, Renegade
Canary Islands	Artemi, Capitan Kidd, Guajiro
Caribbean	Banks, Jeffersons 1785, Jumbie, Martí Mojito Rum, Montego,Plantage Cane Rhum, SpicyGold of the Caribbean, Vizcaya
Colombia	De Caldas, Dictador, Hemingway, Medellin, Punta Cana
Costa Rica	Centenario

Country	Brand
Cuba	Arecha, Caney, Comandante Fidel, Edmundo Dantes, Havana Club
Denmark	Blossa Glögg + Rum
Dominican Republic	Alma de Bohemia, Atlantico, Barcelo, Bermudez, Brugal, Calavera 1492, Conde de Cuba, Dominican Club, Don Rhon Gran Reserva, Dos Ron, Matusalem
Estonia	Vana Tallinn
Ecuador	Christal, Estelar
France	Negrita
Fiji	Seven Tiki
Germany	Asmussen, Dos Ron, Golden Ganja, Pott, Turoa, Westindien Ubersee
Grenada	Plantation
Guadeloupe	Damoiseau, Karukera, Montebello, Musee du Rhum, Coeur de Chauffe, Renegade Guadeloupe Gardel
Guatemala	Botran, Malteco, Zacapa

Rum Guide

Country	Brand
Guyana	Boote Star, Cadenhead Demerara, El Dorado, Lemon Hart, Old Vatted Demerara, Plantation, Port Mourant, Renegade Guyana
Haïti	Barbancourt
India	Old Monk, Old Port, Rancado, Sikkim
Italy	Bombardino Roner
Jamaica	Appleton, Asmussen, Blackwell, Cadenhead Jamaica, Captain Morgan, Coruba, De Kuyper Rum Punch, Denizen (blend met Trinidad rum), Harpoon, Jack Tarr, Koko Kanu, Long Pond, Myers's, Old Captain, Old Jamaica, Plantation, Pott, Renegade, Rum Bar, Sangster's, Sea Wynde, Smith & Cross, Worthy Gold, Wray & Nephew
Madagascar	Dzama
Mallorca	Tunel
Marie Galante	Père Labat
Martinique	Clement, Depaz, Dillon, Duquesne, J.M., La Favorite, La Mauny, Neisson, Saint James, Trois Rivieres
Mauritius	New Grove, Pink Pigeon, White Diamond
Mexico	Mocambo, Xtabentun

Country	Brand
The Netherlands	Barrel Run, Ciguena Carta, De Kuyper Rum Punch, Estaro, Old Captain, Ultimatum Summum, Ultimatum Infinitum, Zuidam Flying Dutchman
Nicaragua	Flor de Cana, Mombacho, Plantation Nicaragua, Zapatera
Panama	Abuelo, Malecon, Ron de Jeremy, Zafra
Paraguay	Papagayo
Peru	Cartavio, Millonario
Philippines	Tanduay, Tondena
Puerto Rico	Bacardi, Blackbeard, Blackheart, Caliche, Captain Morgan, Don Q, Ron Llave, Ronrico
Reunion	Isautier, La Buse, Riviere du Mat, Roquez, Savanna
St. Croix	Captain Morgan, Cruzan, Sailor Jerry
St. Etienne	HSE
St. Kitts & Nevis	Belmont Estate, Brinley
St. Lucia	Admiral Rodney, Bounty, Chairman's Reserve, Elements, Plantation, Renegade, St. Lucia, TOZ
Scotland	Renegade series (for Bruichladdich)
Seychelles	Takamaka Bay
Spain	Arehucas, Captain Marley
South Africa	Jack Tarr, Montego

Country	Brand
Suriname	Black Cat, Borgoe, Marienburg
Sweden	No. 1
Trinidad & Tobago	10Cane, Angostura, Baquba, Kraken, Plantation, Ultimatum
USA	Conch Knockemdown, Prichard's, numerous microdistilleries
Venezuela	Cacique, Diplomatico, Pampero, Santa Teresa

Virgin Islands (GB)

Admiral Nelson, Pusser's, Virgin Gorda, Westindien Ubersee

Virgin Islands (US)

Caribaya, Jolly Roger, Sailor Jerry

Acknowledgements

I would like to thank the following people. They all have contributed to this book, each and every one in his or her own way:

Rick Abdool, Eric Bartels, Jan Beek, Esther & Richard Blesgraaf, Cees Brander, Dave Broom, Gordon Clarke, Birgit Dijkstra, Judith Douglas, Jiska & Tim Ford, Marcel van Gils, Willemien Haagsma, Jennifer Hamilton & little Anna, Blaise Hart, Tony Hart, Peter Heij, Bart Herber, Tina & John Higgenbotham, Willem Huijsman, Robert Hoekstra, Hans Koomen, Dave & Ginny Lovett, Ivo Manca, Dick Meijer, Shunna Gay Mitchell, Piet Molenkamp, Kristine & Louis Nelson, Rius Oerlemans, Becky Lovett Offringa, Sietse Offringa, Thomas Roulston, Frank Ryon, Sandra Seymour, Orvil "Armstrong" Sutherland, Silvia van der Tier, Jochem van den Top, Carsten Vlierboom, Erik Voskamp, Gert Jan van der Weerd, Christine Roby Wilson, Preston Wilson and Ronald Zwartepoorte.

Photo Registry

Bibliography

Books

Barrow, Steve and Peter Dalton. *Reggae The Rough Guide – The Definitive Guide to Jamaican Music from Ska through Roots to Ragga.* 1997 – Rough Guides Ltd. ISBN 1858282470.

Barrow, Steve and Peter Dalton. *The Rough Guide to Reggae – 100 Essential CDs.* 1999 – Rough Guides Ltd. ISBN 9781858285672.

Barty-King, Hugh and Anton Massel. *Rum Yesterday and Today.* 1983 - William Heinemann Ltd. ISBN 9780434452804.

Boon, Ton den e.a. *Klein woordenboek van de Nederlandse taal.* 2007 – Van Dale Lexicografie bv. ISBN 9789066484320.

Bradley, Lloyd. *Bass Culture: When Reggae Was King.* 2001 – Penguin Books. ISBN 9780140237634.

Broom, Dave. *Rum.* 2003 – Octopus Publishing Group Ltd. ISBN 0789208024.

Broom, Dave. *De Barkeepers Bijbel.* 2004 – Het Spectrum BV. ISBN 9027491879.

Craton, Michael and James Walvin. *A Jamaican Plantation: The History of Worthy Park, 1670-1970.* 1970. ISBN 0491002459.

Delevante, Michael P. *Spirits in the Making – A Look at the Basic Characteristics and Manufacturing Methods of Various Types of Alcoholic Beverages.* 2009 – Delevante & Associates, in cooperation with Wray and Nephew. No ISBN.

Foss, Richard. *Rum – A Global History.* 2012 – Reaktion Books Ltd. ISBN 9781861899262.

Gjelten, Tom. *Bacardi and the Long Fight for Cuba.* 2008 – Penguin Books. ISBN 9780670019786.

Mintz, Sidney W. *Sweetness and Power – The Place of Sugar in Modern History.* 1985 – Penguin Books. ISBN 0140092331.

Piggot, Robert - *The Alcohol Textbook*, Chapter 16,17. 4th Ed. 2003 – UK Nottingham University Press. ISBN 1897676131.

White, Timothy. *Catch a Fire.* 2006 – St. Martin's Griffin. ISBN 9780805080865.

Williams, Ian. *Rum – A Social and Sociable History.* 2006 – Nation Books. ISBN 9781560258919.

Bibliography

Steffens, Roger and Peter Simon, *Reggae Scrapbook*. 2007 –
Insight Editions. ISBN 9781933784236.

Films
Jah Rastafari
Marley
Rocksteady: The Roots of Reggae

Websites
Various corporate and musicians websites
Ministryofrum.com
Rum.nl
Rumworld.nl
Suikerhistorie.nl
Wikipedia.org
Youtube.com

Interviews
Beek, Jan. Liquorist, Van Wees, Amersfoort,
the Netherlands.
Broom, Dave. Independent author and drinks journalist,
United Kingdom.
Clarke, Gordon K. Director and Distillery Manager Worthy
Park Estate, Jamaica.
Douglas, Judith. Appleton Academy Ambassador, J. Wray
& Nephew Ltd., Jamaica.
Hart, Blaise. Owner and Managing Director of Good Hope,
Jamaica.

Hart, Tony. Entrepreneur and Owner of Good Hope, Jamaica.

Mitchell, Shunna Gay, aka Sugar. Guide, Appleton Estate Rum Tour, Jamaica.

Nelson, Louis. Research Fellow, The Rothermere American Institute, Oxford University. Associate Professor of Architectural History, University of Virginia.

Roulston, Thomas H.. Distillery Manager J. Wray & Nephew Ltd. (Appleton Estate), Jamaica.

Seymour, Sandra. Operations Manager Appleton Estate Rum Tour, Jamaica.

Vlierboom, Carsten. Managing Director van E&A Scheer BV – Rum blenders. Honorary Consul of Jamaica for the Kingdom of the Netherlands.

Other Works by the Author

English Books

Dutch Books

Het Huis	1997, 2010
Ik kom uit Zwolle, vette pech	2004
Koeboek	1999, 2007
Malts & Jazz *(Deel 1 Drank & Klank Trilogie)*	2012
Men neme Malt	2008
Nightcaps	2007
Rum & Reggae *(Deel 3 Drank & Klank Trilogie)*	2012
Schotse Whisky – The Box: Blended Whisky	2009
Schotse Whisky – The Box: Malt Whisky	
Schotse Whisky – The Box: Proeven van Schotland	
Sint Bonifatiuspark	2008
De Smaak van Whisky	2007
Stokpaardjes	2007
Het Vertrek	2003, 2010
De Weg naar Craigellachie	2004
Whisky Almanak 1e editie & 2de editie	2005 & 2006
Whisky Scheurkalender I & II	2005 & 2007
Whisky & Jazz	2009
De Zes Pijlers van The Macallan	2011
Zwolle, een smakelijk stukje historie	2003

French Books

Classic Malts Selection	2005
Malts & Merveilles	2008

Co-author

Beer Hunter, Whisky Chaser (I. Buxton et al)	2009
Whisky – Eyewitness Guide (C. Maclean et al)	2008
WORLD WHISKY (C Maclean et al)	2009

Other Works by the Author

1001 Whiskies to Try Before You Die
(D. Roskrow et al)   2012
Whisky The World Atlas (D. Broom) (*photos)*   2010

Translated Books

De Malt Whisky Companion (Michael Jackson)   2006
Focus Whisky (Charles Maclean et al)   2008
Whisky de Wereldatlas (Dave Broom)   2011
Whisky Encyclopedie (Michael Jackson)   2005
Single Malt Whisky (David Wishart)   2003
Whisky Geclassificeerd 1e editie (D. Wishart)   2003
Whisky Geclassificeerd 2e editie (D. Wishart)   2006
Whisky Mini Winkler Prins (Carol Shaw)   2003

Articles for newspapers, magazines and websites

Angels Share
Charleston Mercury
InCt
Kiln
Levenswater
WFNN
Whisky Advocate
Whisky Etc.
Whiskyforum
Whisky Magazine
Whisky Pages
Whisky Passion

www.hansoffringa.com

www.ingramcontent.com/pod-product-compliance
Lightning Source LLC
Chambersburg PA
CBHW021926040426
42448CB00008B/927